Still On The Cusp Of Madness
One Day At A Time
Ten Years On

Thank You Jacqui Dyer for ALL your hard Work "Black THRIVE" :o)

Yvonne Stewart-Williams

chipmunkapublishing
the mental health publisher

GW00497573

Yvonne Stewart-Williams

Published by
Chipmunkapublishing
United Kingdom

http://www.chipmunkapublishing.com

Copyright © Yvonne Stewart-Williams 2017

ISBN   978-1-78382-353-6

2

Saturday 28th November 2015

Dear Yvonne,
My beloved sixteen year old son James has just left my abode, after a six hour unsupervised 'quality time' contact session. James is making his way back unescorted to his Looked-After Foster placement; which is located five minutes' walk away. James and I spent our time in doors, his choice, eating McDonald's and watching YouTube videos. I informed my son that Rose, - his long term Social Worker is still off sick and Ingrid, her temporary replacement is also currently off sick; but I met with Jonathan his Social Services' representatives, yesterday, and was given permission for James to arrive at my home at 06:30hrs on Saturday 12th December 2015, so that I can take him to the London School of Gliding, for a day school course of glider flying in Leagraves Bedfordshire. I explained that this is a 2015 Xmas present to him from me. I also told my son that I have obtained consent for his foster carers to apply for his driving licence; so that I can arrange for my son to have a driving lesson on his seventeenth birthday. My son is delighted that I have recently been elected onto the 2015/2016 London Assembly Executive of the Open University Student Association. I am in my second year of a part-time Combined Social Science with Social Policy degree and I although I have recently found out that I have to resit my last exam. I have ambitions of completing a PhD. My son is unsure about my feminism and involvement with the 50:50 Parliament campaigning group for a

more equal gender balance of women members of parliament in the House of Commons. I must say, I can no longer dream of not voting or lending my support to a cause such as this, after lately watching the film: Suffragette. However my son seems to have mixed feeling about my forthcoming 1st December 2015 visit to the House of Commons, Committee Room 14, 50:50 Parliament Debate Commemorating Nancy Astor taking her seat.

Sunday 29th November 2015
Dear Yvonne,
I have just arrived home after a Meeting for Worship, at my local Brixton and Streatham Quaker Friends Meeting House. Today I was on 'Welcoming' duties – Welcoming folk at the door and door duty. I was late arriving to do my service, because I had overslept. I slept for thirteen hours, last night, after taking my 'Stella' Stelazine mental health anti-psychotic sugar-free liquid medication. I have been a member of the British Quakers – Religious Society of Friends for almost two years; after being an attender for twenty-one years. I decided to formally apply to join after the British Quakers discerned that 'Yes', it was right to have 'Same-Sex Equal Marriage'. Now I legally can marry 'C', the love of my life, in England, Scotland and Wales in my religious place of worship. Last year, I was nominated for the post of Quaker Overseer with responsibility for Pastoral Care. I accepted this three year post and participated in a delightful three day Overseers Training in Selly Oak, Birmingham at the Quaker Study Centre in October 2015; although I am unable to visualise

myself as anything other than, Whoopi Goldberg in the film role of 'Sister Act'.

Monday 30th November 2015

Dear Yvonne,

Today at work, I accompanied one of my key-clients to the Design Museum at 28 Shad Thames, near Tower Bridge. It was the first time that I had visited this museum. It was exhibiting mainly bicycles. I was delighted to see a Brompton Cycle on show. I love my job. I have been working full time for Thames Reach the London based Homelessness Charity, in paid employment since the tenth of April 2007 - just over eight and a half years. I started as a Mental Health Floating Support Worker in the borough of Westminster. I was redeployed to my current position, as a Complex Needs and Mental Health Support Worker in a PIE Psychologically Informed Environment Hostel in the borough of Lambeth; on the first of January 2011, on the advice of my psychiatrist after my almost eight week stay as an inmate at Holloway Women's Prison followed by almost three months in SLAM – South London and Maudsley Psychiatric Hospital NHS (National Health Service) Trust. It is 20:00 hrs and my beloved son James has just FaceTimed me, and asked if he can come and see me for an hour. Naturally I said yes, and added that I also need to be at work at 07:00hrs tomorrow morning.

Tuesday 1st December 2015

Dear Yvonne,
Today is World's Aids Day. I wore my red ribbon at work on my 50:50 Parliament T-Shirt. This evening I attended the 50:50 Parliament House of Commons debate to commemorate Nancy Astor taking her seat on 1st Dec 1919. This evening I met and spoke with Frances Scott for the first time. Committee Room 11 was packed and there were people standing listening to the debate. After the debate I bumped into Wes Streeting MP, who also spoke in the debate; along with Cabinet Minister Maria Miller MP, and others including Caroline Lucus MP. This was a cross party non-partisan affair which included a member from a new Women's Party. This evening after giving me a hug, Wes Streeting MP told me to let him know when I am going to be in the House of Commons next, so that he can take me for a cup of tea. I'll try to hold him to it!

Wednesday 2nd December 2015

Dear Yvonne,
This morning I went to collect 'Stella' my anti-psychotic mental health sugar free liquid medication from the pharmacy. They had one bottle and asked me to return for the other three bottles later this week. I then went to my local post office sorting office to collect two books which I ordered on Monday from Amazon: Fateful Triangle – The United States, Israel & the Palestinians by Noam Chomsky. This book is one of my key clients' choice for Xmas 2015, so I ordered one for

him and one for me. I then went shopping in my local M&S Marks & Spencer. Today I also RSVP a place for me for 19:30hrs at the Railway Tavern on the 15th December 2015 for the Dulwich & West Norwood Conservatives Pub Politics. The topic will be Housing. Robert Flint, Lambeth and Southwark Conservative Greater London Assembly Candidate may be attending. I first met and spoke with Robert Flint a few weeks ago, when he was selected to run from us – Conservatives. In addition I have accepted an invitation to attend an OUSA – Open University Student Association to meet with Morris at the Jazz Café in in Foyles on the morning of Friday 18th December 2015.

Thursday 3rd December 2015

Dear Yvonne,
This evening after work, I went to the Fentiman Arms Pub, near the Oval Underground Station; where I attended the pre-Christmas drinks with members and supporters of Vauxhall Conservatives. I enjoyed myself immensely with my colleagues and sipped cups of tea for the evening while speaking with people such as Robert Flint, Lambeth and Southwark, Conservatives GLA Candidate.

Friday 4th December 2015

Dear Yvonne,
As it is my day off today, I started the day with a lie-in. I then did some door to door Coldharbour and Herne Hill Wards postal deliveries of 'The Greater Londoner' newsletter, to support the London Conservative Mayoral Election of Zac Goldsmith and Lambeth and Southwark GLA Robert Flint. I stopped off for my lunch break at The Ritzy in Brixton, where I also obtained my ticket for me to later tonight watch the chemical and gay male documentary film: ChemSex

Saturday 5th December 2015

Dear Yvonne,
The documentary film: ChemSex; was highly thought provoking and I didn't drift off to sleep until approximately 03:00hrs this morning. After a lie-in, this afternoon I dropped in to my local Coldharbour Ward; Brixton Community Base Winter Party, which was being held at the Talma Road Community Centre. In October I had donated sixty pounds cash to Val at no.44 to put towards this Children's Party so that more children would be able to receive a present from the Santas Grotto. After I left the Winter Party, I stopped off at The Ritzy Bar, for a cup of tea and a bite to eat. Then I made my way homeward bound via my local Effra Hall Pub on Rattray Road and stopped there briefly whilst sending Twitter tweets, FaceBook Posts and adjusting my Blog, whilst sipping a glass with full of sparkling water with slices of lemon and lime. When I finally arrived

home I listened to some iTunes downloaded speeches of my much missed mentor Margaret Thatcher and watched the film: The Iron Lady.

Sunday 6th December 2015

Dear Yvonne,
I think it is great news and I am especially pleased that my SoundCloud 50:50 Parliament 1st December 2015 House of Commons recording was accepted by 50:50 Parliament Founder and Director Frances Scott, and is being used. Sadly I failed my latest Open University Social Science exam and will need to re-sit the module; especially as my goal is to pass at PhD Academic Doctorate level.

Monday 7th December 2015

Dear Yvonne,
This morning I collected a parcel from the sorting office for Anthony Hoggard, my neighbour. Anthony is an actor and is currently in a Pantomime in Nottingham, and only returns home on Sundays. Today at work, I accepted Robert Flint, Lambeth & Southwark Conservative GLA – Greater London Assembly Candidate for the 2016 Mayoral Election's. Sunday 20th December 2015 offer to visit me at my Waterloo Homeless Charity, to find out about the work I do.

Tuesday 8th December 2015

Dear Yvonne,
I rang the OU and made arrangements to resume my Combined Social Science degree studies in February 2016, with the module DB123 You, and your money; and the October 2016 module DD206 The Uses of Social Science. Today I wrote to and posted letters to some inactive members of Brixton & Streatham Quaker Friends Meeting House, in my capacity of Overseer with responsibility for their pastoral care. This evening my beloved son James contacted me via FaceTime and we spent some quality time communicating about his EVO car plans. Sadly I won't be having face to face contact with my son on Boxing Day, the 26th December 2015 as he will be spending Xmas and Boxing Day at his male foster carer's brother's home.

Wednesday 9th December 2015

Dear Yvonne,
Today I collected three bottles of 'Stella' anti-psychotic medication from the pharmacy and I started making plans for a 1st January 2016 onwards 'Married Homosexual Men with lived Mental Health Experiences' fundraiser. https://www.gofundme.com/kue7357q The first milestone will be to raise one million pounds to donate to projects. I am going to raise funds by being sponsored to one day at a time, to exercise by riding my Brompton Bicycle and walking more, to get fit and improve MY physical and mental health. I will write a blog, take photos on my

iPhone and using apps like GoFundMe. Strava,
Endomondo and MyFitnessPal. I am also
encouraging folks to lend their financial support
and encouragement by sending me text messages
that I will read and reply to: +44 7490 165136.

Thursday 10th December 2015

Dear Yvonne,
Angela Eagle MP Makes History!!! We do not
share the same Party Politics, but I accept that
yesterday's Wednesday 9th December 2015
House of Commons, PMQs – Prime Minister
Questions, was indeed historic. As openly lesbian
Angela Eagle MP took the place of her Labour
leader, Jeremy Corbyn at the despatch box, in the
absence of Our Prime Minister David Cameron;
who was represented by the Chancellor George
Osborne MP.

Friday 11th December 2015

Dear Yvonne,
Today I spent most of the day in bed on my
iPhone. London Glider School rang me to say
tomorrow's course has been cancelled, due to bad
weather. I rescheduled the course for Saturday
19th December 2015. James contacted me via
FaceTime and then visited me this evening for a
few hours.

Saturday 12th December 2015

Dear Yvonne,
I had a pre-booked face to face contact with James today. We spent our time eating McDonald's while watching a film and then chatting while listening to music. Delightful.

Sunday 13th December 2015

Dear Yvonne,
This morning before work, I visited my dear friend Birgit Rapp in Lewisham. I was only with Birgit for seconds, as I was collecting her Xmas presents to my beloved son James. I am now seriously preparing myself to become a MP – Member of Parliament and take my seat in the House of Commons, Parliament at the next General Election. So far the May 2015 United Kingdom Parliament has 650 MPs. At the next General Election there will be fifty MPs less.

The following are the MPs now seated:
MPs
Find your MP and learn more about MPs.
Members of the House of Commons

Showing 650 out of 650

Surname, First name   Constituency
A   back to top
Abbott, Diane (Labour)
Hackney North and Stoke Newington
Abrahams, Debbie (Labour)

Oldham East and Saddleworth
Adams, Nigel (Conservative)
Selby and Ainsty
Afriyie, Adam (Conservative)
Windsor
Ahmed-Sheikh, Tasmina (Scottish National Party)
        Ochil and South Perthshire
Aldous, Peter (Conservative)
Waveney
Alexander, Heidi (Labour)
Lewisham East
Ali, Rushanara (Labour)
Bethnal Green and Bow
Allan, Lucy (Conservative)
Telford
Allen, Graham (Labour)
Nottingham North
Allen, Heidi (Conservative)
South Cambridgeshire
Amess, David (Conservative)
Southend West
Anderson, David (Labour)
Blaydon
Andrew, Stuart (Conservative)
Pudsey
Ansell, Caroline (Conservative)
Eastbourne
Argar, Edward (Conservative)
Charnwood
Arkless, Richard (Scottish National Party)
Dumfries and Galloway
Ashworth, Jonathan (Labour (Co-op))
Leicester South
Atkins, Victoria (Conservative)

Louth and Horncastle
Austin, Ian (Labour)
Dudley North
B   back to top
Bacon, Richard (Conservative)
South Norfolk
Bailey, Adrian (Labour (Co-op))
West Bromwich West
Baker, Steve (Conservative)
Wycombe
Baldwin, Harriett (Conservative)
West Worcestershire
Barclay, Stephen (Conservative)
North East Cambridgeshire
Bardell, Hannah (Scottish National Party)
Livingston
Baron, John (Conservative)
Basildon and Billericay
Barron, Kevin (Labour)
Rother Valley
Barwell, Gavin (Conservative)
Croydon Central
Bebb, Guto (Conservative)
Aberconwy
Beckett, Margaret (Labour)
Derby South
Bellingham, Henry (Conservative)
North West Norfolk
Benn, Hilary (Labour)
Leeds Central
Benyon, Richard (Conservative)
Newbury
Bercow, John (Speaker)
Buckingham
Beresford, Sir Paul (Conservative)

Mole Valley
Berger, Luciana (Labour (Co-op))
Liverpool, Wavertree
Berry, Jake (Conservative)
Rossendale and Darwen
Berry, James (Conservative)
Kingston and Surbiton
Betts, Clive (Labour)
Sheffield South East
Bingham, Andrew (Conservative)
High Peak
Black, Mhairi (Scottish National Party)
Paisley and Renfrewshire South
Blackford, Ian (Scottish National Party)
Ross, Skye and Lochaber
Blackman, Bob (Conservative)
Harrow East
Blackman, Kirsty (Scottish National Party)
Aberdeen North
Blackman-Woods, Roberta (Labour)
City of Durham
Blackwood, Nicola (Conservative)
Oxford West and Abingdon
Blenkinsop, Tom (Labour)
Middlesbrough South and East Cleveland
Blomfield, Paul (Labour)
Sheffield Central
Blunt, Crispin (Conservative)
Reigate
Boles, Nick (Conservative)
Grantham and Stamford
Bone, Peter (Conservative)
Wellingborough
Borwick, Victoria (Conservative)

Kensington
Boswell, Philip (Scottish National Party)
Coatbridge, Chryston and Bellshill
Bottomley, Sir Peter (Conservative)
Worthing West
Bradley, Karen (Conservative)
Staffordshire Moorlands
Bradshaw, Ben (Labour)
Exeter
Brady, Graham (Conservative)
Altrincham and Sale West
Brady, Mickey (Sinn Fein)
Newry and Armagh
Brake, Tom (Liberal Democrat)
Carshalton and Wallington
Brazier, Julian (Conservative)
Canterbury
Brennan, Kevin (Labour)
Cardiff West
Bridgen, Andrew (Conservative)
North West Leicestershire
Brine, Steve (Conservative)
Winchester
Brock, Deidre (Scottish National Party)
Edinburgh North and Leith
Brokenshire, James (Conservative)
Old Bexley and Sidcup
Brown, Alan (Scottish National Party)
Kilmarnock and Loudoun
Brown, Lyn (Labour)
West Ham
Brown, Nicholas (Labour)
Newcastle upon Tyne East
Bruce, Fiona (Conservative)
Congleton

Bryant, Chris (Labour)
Rhondda
Buck, Karen (Labour)
Westminster North
Buckland, Robert (Conservative)
South Swindon
Burden, Richard (Labour)
Birmingham, Northfield
Burgon, Richard (Labour)
Leeds East
Burnham, Andy (Labour)
Leigh
Burns, Conor (Conservative)
Bournemouth West
Burns, Simon (Conservative)
Chelmsford
Burrowes, David (Conservative)
Enfield, Southgate
Burt, Alistair (Conservative)
North East Bedfordshire
Butler, Dawn (Labour)
Brent Central
Byrne, Liam (Labour)
Birmingham, Hodge Hill
C   back to top
Cadbury, Ruth (Labour)
Brentford and Isleworth
Cairns, Alun (Conservative)
Vale of Glamorgan
Cameron, David (Conservative)
Witney
Cameron, Lisa (Scottish National Party)
East Kilbride, Strathaven and Lesmahagow
Campbell, Alan (Labour)

Tynemouth
Campbell, Gregory (Democratic Unionist Party)
East Londonderry
Campbell, Ronnie (Labour)
Blyth Valley
Carmichael, Alistair (Liberal Democrat)
Orkney and Shetland
Carmichael, Neil (Conservative)
Stroud
Carswell, Douglas (UK Independence Party)
Clacton
Cartlidge, James (Conservative)
South Suffolk
Cash, William (Conservative)
Stone
Caulfield, Maria (Conservative)
Lewes
Chalk, Alex (Conservative)
Cheltenham
Champion, Sarah (Labour)
Rotherham
Chapman, Douglas (Scottish National Party)
Dunfermline and West Fife
Chapman, Jenny (Labour)
Darlington
Cherry, Joanna (Scottish National Party)
Edinburgh South West
Chishti, Rehman (Conservative)
Gillingham and Rainham
Chope, Christopher (Conservative)
Christchurch
Churchill, Jo (Conservative)
Bury St Edmunds
Clark, Greg (Conservative)
Tunbridge Wells

Clarke, Kenneth (Conservative)
Rushcliffe
Clegg, Nick (Liberal Democrat)
Sheffield, Hallam
Cleverly, James (Conservative)
Braintree
Clifton-Brown, Geoffrey(Conservative)
The Cotswolds
Clwyd, Ann (Labour)
Cynon Valley
Coaker, Vernon (Labour)
Gedling
Coffey, Ann (Labour)
Stockport
Coffey, Thérèse (Conservative)
Suffolk Coastal
Collins, Damian (Conservative)
Folkestone and Hythe
Colvile, Oliver (Conservative)
Plymouth, Sutton and Devonport
Cooper, Julie (Labour)
Burnley
Cooper, Rosie (Labour)
West Lancashire
Cooper, Yvette (Labour)
Normanton, Pontefract and Castleford
Corbyn, Jeremy (Labour)
Islington North
Costa, Alberto (Conservative)
South Leicestershire
Cowan, Ronnie (Scottish National Party)
Inverclyde
Cox, Geoffrey (Conservative)
Torridge and West Devon

Cox, Jo (Labour)
Batley and Spen
Coyle, Neil (Labour)
Bermondsey and Old Southwark
Crabb, Stephen (Conservative)
Preseli Pembrokeshire
Crausby, David (Labour)
Bolton North East
Crawley, Angela (Scottish National Party)
Lanark and Hamilton East
Creagh, Mary (Labour)
Wakefield
Creasy, Stella (Labour (Co-op))
Walthamstow
Crouch, Tracey (Conservative)
Chatham and Aylesford
Cruddas, Jon (Labour)
Dagenham and Rainham
Cryer, John (Labour)
Leyton and Wanstead
Cummins, Judith (Labour)
Bradford South
Cunningham, Alex (Labour)
Stockton North
Cunningham, Jim (Labour)
Coventry South
D   back to top
Dakin, Nic (Labour)
Scunthorpe
Danczuk, Simon (Labour)
Rochdale
David, Wayne (Labour)
Caerphilly
Davies, Byron (Conservative)
Gower

Davies, Chris (Conservative)
Brecon and Radnorshire
Davies, David T. C. (Conservative)
Monmouth
Davies, Geraint (Labour (Co-op))
Swansea West
Davies, Glyn (Conservative)
Montgomeryshire
Davies, James (Conservative)
Vale of Clwyd
Davies, Mims (Conservative)
Eastleigh
Davies, Philip (Conservative)
Shipley
Davis, David (Conservative)
Haltemprice and Howden
Day, Martyn (Scottish National Party)
Linlithgow and East Falkirk
De Piero, Gloria (Labour)
Ashfield
Debbonaire, Thangam (Labour)
Bristol West
Dinenage, Caroline (Conservative)
Gosport
Djanogly, Jonathan (Conservative)
Huntingdon
Docherty, Martin John (Scottish National Party)
West Dunbartonshire
Dodds, Nigel (Democratic Unionist Party)
Belfast North
Doherty, Pat (Sinn Fein)
West Tyrone
Donaldson, Jeffrey M. (Democratic Unionist Party)
        Lagan Valley

Donaldson, Stuart Blair (Scottish National Party)
West Aberdeenshire and Kincardine
Donelan, Michelle (Conservative)
Chippenham
Dorries, Nadine (Conservative)
Mid Bedfordshire
Double, Steve (Conservative)
St Austell and Newquay
Doughty, Stephen (Labour (Co-op))
Cardiff South and Penarth
Dowd, Jim (Labour)
Lewisham West and Penge
Dowd, Peter (Labour)
Bootle
Dowden, Oliver (Conservative)
Hertsmere
Doyle-Price, Jackie (Conservative)
Thurrock
Drax, Richard (Conservative)
South Dorset
Dromey, Jack (Labour)
Birmingham, Erdington
Drummond, Flick (Conservative)
Portsmouth South
Duddridge, James (Conservative)
Rochford and Southend East
Dugher, Michael (Labour)
Barnsley East
Duncan, Sir Alan (Conservative)
Rutland and Melton
Duncan Smith, Iain (Conservative)
Chingford and Woodford Green
Dunne, Philip (Conservative)
Ludlow

Durkan, Mark (Social Democratic & Labour Party)
     Foyle
E   back to top
Eagle, Angela (Labour)
Wallasey
Eagle, Maria (Labour)
Garston and Halewood
Edwards, Jonathan (Plaid Cymru)
Carmarthen East and Dinefwr
Efford, Clive (Labour)
Eltham
Elliott, Julie (Labour)
Sunderland Central
Elliott, Tom (Ulster Unionist Party)
Fermanagh and South Tyrone
Ellis, Michael (Conservative)
Northampton North
Ellison, Jane (Conservative)
Battersea
Ellman, Louise (Labour (Co-op))
Liverpool, Riverside
Ellwood, Tobias (Conservative)
Bournemouth East
Elphicke, Charlie (Conservative)
Dover
Engel, Natascha (Labour)
North East Derbyshire
Esterson, Bill (Labour)
Sefton Central
Eustice, George (Conservative)
Camborne and Redruth
Evans, Chris (Labour (Co-op))
Islwyn
Evans, Graham (Conservative)

Weaver Vale
Evans, Nigel (Conservative)
Ribble Valley
Evennett, David (Conservative)
Bexleyheath and Crayford
F   back to top
Fabricant, Michael (Conservative)
Lichfield
Fallon, Michael (Conservative)
Sevenoaks
Farrelly, Paul (Labour)
Newcastle-under-Lyme
Farron, Tim (Liberal Democrat)
Westmorland and Lonsdale
Fellows, Marion (Scottish National Party)
Motherwell and Wishaw
Fernandes, Suella (Conservative)
Fareham
Ferrier, Margaret (Scottish National Party)
Rutherglen and Hamilton West
Field, Frank (Labour)
Birkenhead
Field, Mark (Conservative)
Cities of London and Westminster
Fitzpatrick, Jim (Labour)
Poplar and Limehouse
Flello, Robert (Labour)
Stoke-on-Trent South
Fletcher, Colleen (Labour)
Coventry North East
Flint, Caroline (Labour)
Don Valley
Flynn, Paul (Labour)
Newport West
Foster, Kevin (Conservative)

Torbay
Fovargue, Yvonne (Labour)
Makerfield
Fox, Liam (Conservative)
North Somerset
Foxcroft, Vicky (Labour)
Lewisham, Deptford
Francois, Mark (Conservative)
Rayleigh and Wickford
Frazer, Lucy (Conservative)
South East Cambridgeshire
Freeman, George (Conservative)
Mid Norfolk
Freer, Mike (Conservative)
Finchley and Golders Green
Fuller, Richard (Conservative)
Bedford
Fysh, Marcus (Conservative)
Yeovil
G   back to top
Gale, Sir Roger (Conservative)
North Thanet
Gapes, Mike (Labour (Co-op))
Ilford South
Gardiner, Barry (Labour)
Brent North
Garnier, Mark (Conservative)
Wyre Forest
Garnier, Sir Edward (Conservative)
Harborough
Gauke, David (Conservative)
South West Hertfordshire
Gethins, Stephen (Scottish National Party)
North East Fife

Ghani, Nusrat (Conservative)
Wealden
Gibb, Nick (Conservative)
Bognor Regis and Littlehampton
Gibson, Patricia (Scottish National Party)
North Ayrshire and Arran
Gillan, Cheryl (Conservative)
Chesham and Amersham
Glass, Pat (Labour)
North West Durham
Glen, John (Conservative)
Salisbury
Glindon, Mary (Labour)
North Tyneside
Godsiff, Roger (Labour)
Birmingham, Hall Green
Goldsmith, Zac (Conservative)
Richmond Park
Goodman, Helen (Labour)
Bishop Auckland
Goodwill, Robert (Conservative)
Scarborough and Whitby
Gove, Michael (Conservative)
Surrey Heath
Grady, Patrick (Scottish National Party)
Glasgow North
Graham, Richard (Conservative)
Gloucester
Grant, Helen (Conservative)
Maidstone and The Weald
Grant, Peter (Scottish National Party)
Glenrothes
Gray, James (Conservative)
North Wiltshire
Gray, Neil (Scottish National Party)

Airdrie and Shotts
Grayling, Chris (Conservative)
Epsom and Ewell
Green, Chris (Conservative)
Bolton West
Green, Damian (Conservative)
Ashford
Green, Kate (Labour)
Stretford and Urmston
Greening, Justine (Conservative)
Putney
Greenwood, Lilian (Labour)
Nottingham South
Greenwood, Margaret (Labour)
Wirral West
Grieve, Dominic (Conservative)
Beaconsfield
Griffith, Nia (Labour)
Llanelli
Griffiths, Andrew (Conservative)
Burton
Gummer, Ben (Conservative)
Ipswich
Gwynne, Andrew (Labour)
Denton and Reddish
Gyimah, Sam (Conservative)
East Surrey
H   back to top
Haigh, Louise (Labour)
Sheffield, Heeley
Halfon, Robert (Conservative)
Harlow
Hall, Luke (Conservative)
Thornbury and Yate

Hamilton, Fabian (Labour)
Leeds North East
Hammond, Philip (Conservative)
Runnymede and Weybridge
Hammond, Stephen (Conservative)
Wimbledon
Hancock, Matthew (Conservative)
West Suffolk
Hands, Greg (Conservative)
Chelsea and Fulham
Hanson, David (Labour)
Delyn
Harman, Harriet (Labour)
Camberwell and Peckham
Harper, Mark (Conservative)
Forest of Dean
Harpham, Harry (Labour)
Sheffield, Brightside and Hillsborough
Harrington, Richard (Conservative)
Watford
Harris, Carolyn (Labour)
Swansea East
Harris, Rebecca (Conservative)
Castle Point
Hart, Simon (Conservative)
Carmarthen West and South Pembrokeshire
Haselhurst, Sir Alan (Conservative)
Saffron Walden
Hayes, Helen (Labour)
Dulwich and West Norwood
Hayes, John (Conservative)
South Holland and The Deepings
Hayman, Sue (Labour)
Workington
Heald, Sir Oliver (Conservative)

North East Hertfordshire
Healey, John (Labour)
Wentworth and Dearne
Heappey, James (Conservative)
Wells
Heaton-Harris, Chris (Conservative)
Daventry
Heaton-Jones, Peter (Conservative)
North Devon
Henderson, Gordon (Conservative)
Sittingbourne and Sheppey
Hendrick, Mark (Labour (Co-op))
Preston
Hendry, Drew (Scottish National Party)
Inverness, Nairn, Badenoch and Strathspey
Hepburn, Stephen (Labour)
Jarrow
Herbert, Nick (Conservative)
Arundel and South Downs
Hermon, Lady (Independent)
North Down
Hillier, Meg (Labour (Co-op))
Hackney South and Shoreditch
Hinds, Damian (Conservative)
East Hampshire
Hoare, Simon (Conservative)
North Dorset
Hodge, Margaret (Labour)
Barking
Hodgson, Sharon (Labour)
Washington and Sunderland West
Hoey, Kate (Labour)
Vauxhall
Hollern, Kate (Labour)

Blackburn
Hollingbery, George (Conservative)
Meon Valley
Hollinrake, Kevin (Conservative)
Thirsk and Malton
Hollobone, Philip (Conservative)
Kettering
Holloway, Adam (Conservative)
Gravesham
Hopkins, Kelvin (Labour)
Luton North
Hopkins, Kris (Conservative)
Keighley
Hosie, Stewart (Scottish National Party)
Dundee East
Howarth, George (Labour)
Knowsley
Howarth, Sir Gerald (Conservative)
Aldershot
Howell, John (Conservative)
Henley
Howlett, Ben (Conservative)
Bath
Hoyle, Lindsay (Labour)
Chorley
Huddleston, Nigel (Conservative)
Mid Worcestershire
Hunt, Jeremy (Conservative)
South West Surrey
Hunt, Tristram (Labour)
Stoke-on-Trent Central
Huq, Rupa (Labour)
Ealing Central and Acton
Hurd, Nick (Conservative)
Ruislip, Northwood and Pinner

Hussain, Imran (Labour)
Bradford East
I   back to top
Irranca-Davies, Huw (Labour)
Ogmore
J   back to top
Jackson, Stewart (Conservative)
Peterborough
James, Margot (Conservative)
Stourbridge
Jarvis, Dan (Labour)
Barnsley Central
Javid, Sajid (Conservative)
Bromsgrove
Jayawardena, Ranil (Conservative)
North East Hampshire
Jenkin, Bernard (Conservative)
Harwich and North Essex
Jenkyns, Andrea (Conservative)
Morley and Outwood
Jenrick, Robert (Conservative)
Newark
Johnson, Alan (Labour)
Kingston upon Hull West and Hessle
Johnson, Boris (Conservative)
Uxbridge and South Ruislip
Johnson, Diana (Labour)
Kingston upon Hull North
Johnson, Gareth (Conservative)
Dartford
Johnson, Joseph (Conservative)
Orpington
Jones, Andrew (Conservative)
Harrogate and Knaresborough

Jones, David (Conservative)
Clwyd West
Jones, Gerald (Labour)
Merthyr Tydfil and Rhymney
Jones, Graham (Labour)
Hyndburn
Jones, Helen (Labour)
Warrington North
Jones, Kevan (Labour)
North Durham
Jones, Marcus (Conservative)
Nuneaton
Jones, Susan Elan (Labour)
Clwyd South
K   back to top
Kane, Mike (Labour)
Wythenshawe and Sale East
Kaufman, Sir Gerald (Labour)
Manchester, Gorton
Kawczynski, Daniel (Conservative)
Shrewsbury and Atcham
Keeley, Barbara (Labour)
Worsley and Eccles South
Kendall, Liz (Labour)
Leicester West
Kennedy, Seema (Conservative)
South Ribble
Kerevan, George (Scottish National Party)
East Lothian
Kerr, Calum (Scottish National Party)
Berwickshire, Roxburgh and Selkirk
Khan, Sadiq (Labour)
Tooting
Kinahan, Danny (Ulster Unionist Party)
South Antrim

Kinnock, Stephen (Labour)
Aberavon
Kirby, Simon (Conservative)
Brighton, Kemptown
Knight, Julian (Conservative)
Solihull
Knight, Sir Greg (Conservative)
East Yorkshire
Kwarteng, Kwasi (Conservative)
Spelthorne
Kyle, Peter (Labour)
Hove
L   back to top
Laing, Eleanor (Conservative)
Epping Forest
Lamb, Norman (Liberal Democrat)
North Norfolk
Lammy, David (Labour)
Tottenham
Lancaster, Mark (Conservative)
Milton Keynes North
Latham, Pauline (Conservative)
Mid Derbyshire
Lavery, Ian (Labour)
Wansbeck
Law, Chris (Scottish National Party)
Dundee West
Leadsom, Andrea (Conservative)
South Northamptonshire
Lee, Phillip (Conservative)
Bracknell
Lefroy, Jeremy (Conservative)
Stafford
Leigh, Sir Edward (Conservative)

Gainsborough
Leslie, Charlotte (Conservative)
Bristol North West
Leslie, Chris (Labour (Co-op))
Nottingham East
Letwin, Oliver (Conservative)
West Dorset
Lewell-Buck, Emma (Labour)
South Shields
Lewis, Brandon (Conservative)
Great Yarmouth
Lewis, Clive (Labour)
Norwich South
Lewis, Ivan (Labour)
Bury South
Lewis, Julian (Conservative)
New Forest East
Liddell-Grainger, Ian (Conservative)
Bridgwater and West Somerset
Lidington, David (Conservative)
Aylesbury
Lilley, Peter (Conservative)
Hitchin and Harpenden
Long Bailey, Rebecca (Labour)
Salford and Eccles
Lopresti, Jack (Conservative)
Filton and Bradley Stoke
Lord, Jonathan (Conservative)
Woking
Loughton, Tim (Conservative)
East Worthing and Shoreham
Lucas, Caroline (Green Party)
Brighton, Pavilion
Lucas, Ian C. (Labour)
Wrexham

Lumley, Karen (Conservative)
Redditch
Lynch, Holly (Labour)
Halifax
M   back to top
Mc Nally, John (Scottish National Party)
Falkirk
McCabe, Steve (Labour)
Birmingham, Selly Oak
McCaig, Callum (Scottish National Party)
Aberdeen South
McCarthy, Kerry (Labour)
Bristol East
McCartney, Jason (Conservative)
Colne Valley
McCartney, Karl (Conservative)
Lincoln
McDonagh, Siobhain (Labour)
Mitcham and Morden
McDonald, Andy (Labour)
Middlesbrough
McDonald, Stewart Malcolm(Scottish National
Party) Glasgow South
McDonald, Stuart C. (Scottish National Party)
Cumbernauld, Kilsyth and Kirkintilloch East
McDonnell, Alasdair (Social Democratic & Labour
Party) Belfast South
McDonnell, John (Labour)
Hayes and Harlington
McFadden, Pat (Labour)
Wolverhampton South East
McGarry, Natalie (Independent)
Glasgow East
McGinn, Conor (Labour)

St Helens North
McGovern, Alison (Labour)
Wirral South
McInnes, Liz (Labour)
Heywood and Middleton
Mackinlay, Craig (Conservative)
South Thanet
McKinnell, Catherine (Labour)
Newcastle upon Tyne North
Mackintosh, David (Conservative)
Northampton South
McLaughlin, Anne (Scottish National Party)
Glasgow North East
McLoughlin, Patrick (Conservative)
Derbyshire Dales
McMahon, Jim (Labour)
Oldham West and Royton
MacNeil, Angus Brendan (Scottish National Party)
      Na h-Eileanan an Iar
McPartland, Stephen (Conservative)
Stevenage
Mactaggart, Fiona (Labour)
Slough
Madders, Justin (Labour)
Ellesmere Port and Neston
Mahmood, Khalid (Labour)
Birmingham, Perry Barr
Mahmood, Shabana (Labour)
Birmingham, Ladywood
Main, Anne (Conservative)
St Albans
Mak, Alan (Conservative)
Havant
Malhotra, Seema (Labour (Co-op))
Feltham and Heston

Malthouse, Kit (Conservative)
North West Hampshire
Mann, John (Labour)
Bassetlaw
Mann, Scott (Conservative)
North Cornwall
Marris, Rob (Labour)
Wolverhampton South West
Marsden, Gordon (Labour)
Blackpool South
Maskell, Rachael (Labour (Co-op))
York Central
Maskey, Paul (Sinn Fein)
Belfast West
Matheson, Christian (Labour)
City of Chester
Mathias, Tania (Conservative)
Twickenham
May, Theresa (Conservative)
Maidenhead
Maynard, Paul (Conservative)
Blackpool North and Cleveleys
Meale, Sir Alan (Labour)
Mansfield
Mearns, Ian (Labour)
Gateshead
Menzies, Mark (Conservative)
Fylde
Mercer, Johnny (Conservative)
Plymouth, Moor View
Merriman, Huw (Conservative)
Bexhill and Battle
Metcalfe, Stephen (Conservative)
South Basildon and East Thurrock

Miliband, Edward (Labour)
Doncaster North
Miller, Maria (Conservative)
Basingstoke
Milling, Amanda (Conservative)
Cannock Chase
Mills, Nigel (Conservative)
Amber Valley
Milton, Anne (Conservative)
Guildford
Mitchell, Andrew (Conservative)
Sutton Coldfield
Molloy, Francie (Sinn Fein)
Mid Ulster
Monaghan, Carol (Scottish National Party)
Glasgow North West
Monaghan, Paul (Scottish National Party)
Caithness, Sutherland and Easter Ross
Moon, Madeleine (Labour)
Bridgend
Mordaunt, Penny (Conservative)
Portsmouth North
Morden, Jessica (Labour)
Newport East
Morgan, Nicky (Conservative)
Loughborough
Morris, Anne Marie (Conservative)
Newton Abbot
Morris, David (Conservative)
Morecambe and Lunesdale
Morris, Grahame (Labour)
Easington
Morris, James (Conservative)
Halesowen and Rowley Regis
Morton, Wendy (Conservative)

Aldridge-Brownhills
Mowat, David (Conservative)
Warrington South
Mulholland, Greg (Liberal Democrat)
Leeds North West
Mullin, Roger (Scottish National Party)
Kirkcaldy and Cowdenbeath
Mundell, David (Conservative)
Dumfriesshire, Clydesdale and Tweeddale
Murray, Ian (Labour)
Edinburgh South
Murray, Sheryll (Conservative)
South East Cornwall
Murrison, Andrew (Conservative)
South West Wiltshire
N   back to top
Nandy, Lisa (Labour)
Wigan
Neill, Robert (Conservative)
Bromley and Chislehurst
Newlands, Gavin (Scottish National Party)
Paisley and Renfrewshire North
Newton, Sarah (Conservative)
Truro and Falmouth
Nicolson, John (Scottish National Party)
East Dunbartonshire
Nokes, Caroline (Conservative)
Romsey and Southampton North
Norman, Jesse (Conservative)
Hereford and South Herefordshire
Nuttall, David (Conservative)
Bury North
O   back to top
Offord, Matthew (Conservative)

Hendon
O'Hara, Brendan (Scottish National Party)
Argyll and Bute
Onn, Melanie (Labour)
Great Grimsby
Onwurah, Chi (Labour)
Newcastle upon Tyne Central
Opperman, Guy (Conservative)
Hexham
Osamor, Kate (Labour (Co-op))
Edmonton
Osborne, George (Conservative)
Tatton
Oswald, Kirsten (Scottish National Party)
East Renfrewshire
Owen, Albert (Labour)
Ynys Môn
P   back to top
Paisley, Ian (Democratic Unionist Party)
North Antrim
Parish, Neil (Conservative)
Tiverton and Honiton
Patel, Priti (Conservative)
Witham
Paterson, Owen (Conservative)
North Shropshire
Paterson, Steven (Scottish National Party)
Stirling
Pawsey, Mark (Conservative)
Rugby
Pearce, Teresa (Labour)
Erith and Thamesmead
Penning, Mike (Conservative)
Hemel Hempstead
Pennycook, Matthew (Labour)

Greenwich and Woolwich
Penrose, John (Conservative)
Weston-super-Mare
Percy, Andrew (Conservative)
Brigg and Goole
Perkins, Toby (Labour)
Chesterfield
Perry, Claire (Conservative)
Devizes
Phillips, Jess (Labour)
Birmingham, Yardley
Phillips, Stephen (Conservative)
Sleaford and North Hykeham
Phillipson, Bridget (Labour)
Houghton and Sunderland South
Philp, Chris (Conservative)
Croydon South
Pickles, Eric (Conservative)
Brentwood and Ongar
Pincher, Christopher (Conservative)
Tamworth
Poulter, Dr (Conservative)
Central Suffolk and North Ipswich
Pound, Stephen (Labour)
Ealing North
Pow, Rebecca (Conservative)
Taunton Deane
Powell, Lucy (Labour (Co-op))
Manchester Central
Prentis, Victoria (Conservative)
Banbury
Prisk, Mark (Conservative)
Hertford and Stortford
Pritchard, Mark (Conservative)

The Wrekin
Pugh, John (Liberal Democrat)
Southport
Pursglove, Tom (Conservative)
Corby
Q   back to top
Quin, Jeremy (Conservative)
Horsham
Quince, Will (Conservative)
Colchester
Qureshi, Yasmin (Labour)
Bolton South East
R   back to top
Raab, Dominic (Conservative)
Esher and Walton
Rayner, Angela (Labour)
Ashton-under-Lyne
Redwood, John (Conservative)
Wokingham
Reed, Jamie (Labour)
Copeland
Reed, Steve (Labour (Co-op))
Croydon North
Rees, Christina (Labour)
Neath
Rees-Mogg, Jacob (Conservative)
North East Somerset
Reeves, Rachel (Labour)
Leeds West
Reynolds, Emma (Labour)
Wolverhampton North East
Reynolds, Jonathan (Labour (Co-op))
Stalybridge and Hyde
Rimmer, Marie (Labour)
St Helens South and Whiston

Ritchie, Margaret (Social Democratic & Labour Party) South Down
Robertson, Angus (Scottish National Party) Moray
Robertson, Laurence (Conservative) Tewkesbury
Robinson, Gavin (Democratic Unionist Party) Belfast East
Robinson, Geoffrey (Labour) Coventry North West
Robinson, Mary (Conservative) Cheadle
Rosindell, Andrew (Conservative) Romford
Rotheram, Steve (Labour) Liverpool, Walton
Rudd, Amber (Conservative) Hastings and Rye
Rutley, David (Conservative) Macclesfield
Ryan, Joan (Labour) Enfield North
S   back to top
Salmond, Alex (Scottish National Party) Gordon
Sandbach, Antoinette(Conservative) Eddisbury
Saville Roberts, Liz (Plaid Cymru) Dwyfor Meirionnydd
Scully, Paul (Conservative) Sutton and Cheam
Selous, Andrew (Conservative) South West Bedfordshire
Shah, Naz (Labour)

Bradford West
Shannon, Jim (Democratic Unionist Party)
Strangford
Shapps, Grant (Conservative)
Welwyn Hatfield
Sharma, Alok (Conservative)
Reading West
Sharma, Virendra (Labour)
Ealing, Southall
Sheerman, Barry (Labour (Co-op))
Huddersfield
Shelbrooke, Alec (Conservative)
Elmet and Rothwell
Sheppard, Tommy (Scottish National Party)
Edinburgh East
Sherriff, Paula (Labour)
Dewsbury
Shuker, Gavin (Labour (Co-op))
Luton South
Siddiq, Tulip (Labour)
Hampstead and Kilburn
Simpson, David (Democratic Unionist Party)
Upper Bann
Simpson, Keith (Conservative)
Broadland
Skidmore, Chris (Conservative)
Kingswood
Skinner, Dennis (Labour)
Bolsover
Slaughter, Andy (Labour)
Hammersmith
Smeeth, Ruth (Labour)
Stoke-on-Trent North
Smith, Andrew (Labour)
Oxford East

Smith, Angela (Labour)
Penistone and Stocksbridge
Smith, Cat (Labour)
Lancaster and Fleetwood
Smith, Chloe (Conservative)
Norwich North
Smith, Henry (Conservative)
Crawley
Smith, Jeff (Labour)
Manchester, Withington
Smith, Julian (Conservative)
Skipton and Ripon
Smith, Nick (Labour)
Blaenau Gwent
Smith, Owen (Labour)
Pontypridd
Smith, Royston (Conservative)
Southampton, Itchen
Smyth, Karin (Labour)
Bristol South
Soames, Sir Nicholas(Conservative)
Mid Sussex
Solloway, Amanda (Conservative)
Derby North
Soubry, Anna (Conservative)
Broxtowe
Spellar, John (Labour)
Warley
Spelman, Caroline (Conservative)
Meriden
Spencer, Mark (Conservative)
Sherwood
Starmer, Keir (Labour)
Holborn and St Pancras

Stephens, Chris (Scottish National Party)
Glasgow South West
Stephenson, Andrew (Conservative)
Pendle
Stevens, Jo (Labour)
Cardiff Central
Stevenson, John (Conservative)
Carlisle
Stewart, Bob (Conservative)
Beckenham
Stewart, Iain (Conservative)
Milton Keynes South
Stewart, Rory (Conservative)
Penrith and The Border
Streeter, Gary (Conservative)
South West Devon
Streeting, Wes (Labour)
Ilford North
Stride, Mel (Conservative)
Central Devon
Stringer, Graham (Labour)
Blackley and Broughton
Stuart, Gisela (Labour)
Birmingham, Edgbaston
Stuart, Graham (Conservative)
Beverley and Holderness
Sturdy, Julian (Conservative)
York Outer
Sunak, Rishi (Conservative)
Richmond (Yorks)
Swayne, Desmond (Conservative)
New Forest West
Swire, Hugo (Conservative)
East Devon
Syms, Robert (Conservative)

Poole
T   back to top
Tami, Mark (Labour)
Alyn and Deeside
Thewliss, Alison (Scottish National Party)
Glasgow Central
Thomas, Derek (Conservative)
St Ives
Thomas, Gareth (Labour (Co-op))
Harrow West
Thomas-Symonds, Nick (Labour)
Torfaen
Thompson, Owen (Scottish National Party)
Midlothian
Thomson, Michelle (Independent)
Edinburgh West
Thornberry, Emily (Labour)
Islington South and Finsbury
Throup, Maggie (Conservative)
Erewash
Timms, Stephen (Labour)
East Ham
Timpson, Edward (Conservative)
Crewe and Nantwich
Tolhurst, Kelly (Conservative)
Rochester and Strood
Tomlinson, Justin (Conservative)
North Swindon
Tomlinson, Michael (Conservative)
Mid Dorset and North Poole
Tracey, Craig (Conservative)
North Warwickshire
Tredinnick, David (Conservative)
Bosworth

Trevelyan, Anne-Marie(Conservative)
Berwick-upon-Tweed
Trickett, Jon (Labour)
Hemsworth
Truss, Elizabeth (Conservative)
South West Norfolk
Tugendhat, Tom (Conservative)
Tonbridge and Malling
Turley, Anna (Labour (Co-op))
Redcar
Turner, Andrew (Conservative)
Isle of Wight
Turner, Karl (Labour)
Kingston upon Hull East
Twigg, Derek (Labour)
Halton
Twigg, Stephen (Labour (Co-op))
Liverpool, West Derby
Tyrie, Andrew (Conservative)
Chichester
U   back to top
Umunna, Chuka (Labour)
Streatham
V   back to top
Vaizey, Edward (Conservative)
Wantage
Vara, Shailesh (Conservative)
North West Cambridgeshire
Vaz, Keith (Labour)
Leicester East
Vaz, Valerie (Labour)
Walsall South
Vickers, Martin (Conservative)
Cleethorpes
Villiers, Theresa (Conservative)

Chipping Barnet
W   back to top
Walker, Charles (Conservative)
Broxbourne
Walker, Robin (Conservative)
Worcester
Wallace, Ben (Conservative)
Wyre and Preston North
Warburton, David (Conservative)
Somerton and Frome
Warman, Matt (Conservative)
Boston and Skegness
Watkinson, Dame Angela(Conservative)
Hornchurch and Upminster
Watson, Tom (Labour)
West Bromwich East
Weir, Mike (Scottish National Party)
Angus
West, Catherine (Labour)
Hornsey and Wood Green
Wharton, James (Conservative)
Stockton South
Whately, Helen (Conservative)
Faversham and Mid Kent
Wheeler, Heather (Conservative)
South Derbyshire
White, Chris (Conservative)
Warwick and Leamington
Whiteford, Eilidh (Scottish National Party)
Banff and Buchan
Whitehead, Alan (Labour)
Southampton, Test
Whitford, Philippa (Scottish National Party)
Central Ayrshire

Whittaker, Craig (Conservative)
Calder Valley
Whittingdale, John (Conservative)
Maldon
Wiggin, Bill (Conservative)
North Herefordshire
Williams, Craig (Conservative)
Cardiff North
Williams, Hywel (Plaid Cymru)
Arfon
Williams, Mark (Liberal Democrat)
Ceredigion
Williamson, Gavin (Conservative)
South Staffordshire
Wilson, Corri (Scottish National Party)
Ayr, Carrick and Cumnock
Wilson, Phil (Labour)
Sedgefield
Wilson, Rob (Conservative)
Reading East
Wilson, Sammy (Democratic Unionist Party)
East Antrim
Winnick, David (Labour)
Walsall North
Winterton, Rosie (Labour)
Doncaster Central
Wishart, Pete (Scottish National Party)
Perth and North Perthshire
Wollaston, Sarah (Conservative)
Totnes
Wood, Mike (Conservative)
Dudley South
Woodcock, John (Labour (Co-op))
Barrow and Furness
Wragg, William (Conservative)

Hazel Grove
Wright, Iain (Labour)
Hartlepool
Wright, Jeremy (Conservative)
Kenilworth and Southam
Z   back to top
Zahawi, Nadhim (Conservative)
Stratford-on-Avon
Zeichner, Daniel (Labour)
Cambridge

Monday 14th December 2015

Dear Yvonne,
I my favourite lesbian fiction writer is Karin
Kallmaker. I have read and almost all of her
books. I am currently reading Karin's novella
'Comfort and Joy' on my kindle. My events for this
week are: Today – I am attending the 2015
Stonewall UK Volunteers Xmas Party.
Tuesday – I am attending the Local Politics event
of Dulwich & West Norwood Conservatives, Pub
Politics – the topic is: - Housing.
Friday – I meet with my Open University Student
Association London Assembly Executive
colleagues.
Saturday – I attend the London Gliding School
with my beloved son James.
Sunday – I attend a Brixton & Streatham Quaker
Meeting for Worship, followed by an Overseers
Meeting. In addition I will host Robert Flint at my
Waterloo Homeless Charity project, near Coin
Street Neighbourhood Centre; and induct him into
the nature of my work.

Monday 14th December 2015

Dear Yvonne,
This evening I had a wonderful time at the 2015
Stonewall UK Xmas party for Volunteers. I sipped
my drink of sprite while I spoke with Louise and
Roy.

Tuesday 15th December 2015

Dear Yvonne,
This evening, I enjoyed a wonderfully delightful
evening at the Pub Politics event with my Dulwich
and West Norwood Conservatives at the Railway
Pub in Tulse Hill. I officially launched my bid to
become the first black openly lesbian Tory MP to
take my seat at the next General Election for the
Dulwich and West Norwood Conservatives. This
evening I purchase train tickets for the journey to
the London Gliding School.

Wednesday 16th December 2015

Dear Yvonne,
Today I had a client day at my Waterloo Homeless
Charity.

Thursday 17th December 2015

Dear Yvonne,
This morning I had a lie-in.

Friday 18th December 2015

Dear Yvonne,
This evening my beloved son James visited me to complete some forms. I informed him that we will need to phone London Gliding School tomorrow morning.

Saturday 19th December 2015

Dear Yvonne,
This morning my beloved son James arrived at 07:30am. I rang London Gliding School at 08:30hrs and was told James' flight today has been cancelled. James and I spent the day together.

Sunday 20th December 2015

Dear Yvonne,
Today I attended Meeting for Worship at my local Brixton & Streatham Quaker Friends Meeting House. Then after drinking a cup of tea and chatting with attenders and members; I attended a Quaker Overseers Meeting. At 4pm this afternoon, I received Rob as a guest at my 73 Stamford Street Waterloo Homeless Charity. Rob met a few of my colleagues and clients and toured the hostel whilst I explained my work to him. I introduced

Rob as Robert Flint, Lambeth and Southwark Conservative London Assembly Candidate for the 2016 London Mayoral Election. Rob, who is also a professional lawyer took photos with me. Rob left my place of work at 18:00hrs and later this evening I received an email from Rob thanking me and giving me an invitation for dinner.

Monday 21st December 2015

Dear Yvonne,
Just for today, I am grateful and blessed.

Tuesday 22nd December 2015

Dear Yvonne,
Today I received my monthly salary from my Waterloo Homeless Charity at 73 Stamford St. I paid my Housing Co-operative rent via my online banking app. Then visited my bank to change my standing order. I also paid the following montly instalment via PayPoint: Thames Water rates, Television Licence, British Gas. I paid a contribution to EDF – Electricity using an old bill. I paid twenty pounds towards my Monthly mobile phone cost. I visited The Ritzy Bar and bought a ticket for one to watch the film: Star Wars – The Force Awakens – tonight at 21:10 – in fact I used one of my free tickets which comes with membership of The Ritzy. Finally I went food shopping at M&S in Brixton. On my return home, I made myself a bite to eat and had a cup of tea. Washed my clothes and had a lovely long candlelit aromatherapy hot bubble bath; while listening to

BBC Radio Four through my wireless waterproof speaker. Finally I went to bed and slept for ninety minutes in preparation for the film.

Wednesday 23rd December 2015

Dear Yvonne,
Today I donated twenty-five pounds to the Electoral Reform Society via PayPal. I instructed ERS to use the monies towards Women Representatives.

Thursday 24th December 2015

Dear Yvonne,
Today I my last working day before Xmas 2015. Tomorrow I am wearing a Santa Hat and a Stonewall UK, Some Guys, Marry Guys. Get Over It! T-Shirt to my local Brixton & Streatham Quaker Meeting for Worship followed by my day at the NA – Narcotics Anonymous Xmas Dinner at the Oval. However Just for today I am wearing my Bar – Humbug hat with my Stonewall Some People are Trans. Get Over It! T-Shirt.

2015 Xmas Day

Dear Yvonne,
Today I had a Wonderful time going to a meeting, committing to Service and dinning at the Oval in Lambeth with NA-Narcotics Anonymous for the No One is Alone 2015 Dinner.

Saturday 26 December 2015

Dear Yvonne,
Today is Boxing Day. I am Ironing my Stonewall UK T-Shirts…

Sunday 27 December 2015

Dear Yvonne,
I bought one ticket for me to watch the film: Sherlock Holmes. This film will star Benedict Cumberbatch at The Ritzy Bar in Brixton on Friday 1 January 2016.

Monday 28 December 2015

Dear Yvonne,
Today is a Bank Holiday in England. I worked at my 73 Stamford Street, Thames Reach Homeless Charity Waterloo paid employment.

Tuesday 29 December 2015

Dear Yvonne,
My beloved son spoke with me via Apple FaceTime and visited me for one hour. We dined on McDonalds.

Wednesday 30 December 2015

Dear Yvonne,
Today I worked a late shift and arrived home just before mid-night.

Thursday 31st December 2015

Dear Yvonne,
Jeremy Swain, Chief Executive of Thames Reach is leading on Dry January 2016. I have spoken to a few of my clients and there has been a commitment to try to remain alcohol free for the whole month of January, one day at a time. This evening I downloaded the Logic Pro X app onto my Apple MacBook Computer. In addition, I ordered an Apple iPad Pro.

Friday 1st January 2016

Dear Yvonne,
I welcomed the 2016 New Year in seated in my local Effra Hall pub, in Rattray Road, Brixton. I sat under a large screen television, listening to loud music and sipped sparkling bottled water with slices of lime and lemon; whilst on reading twitter tweets and an Amazon kindle ebook on my iPhone. I walked home to the sights and sounds of fireworks. As I approached my front door, some neighbours - a woman with a man and a girl child appeared to be watching the fireworks display at their front door. The women gave me a hug and kissed me on both cheeks. Once home, I had a wonderful relaxing hot scented candlelit bubble bath and listened to BBC Radio Four. Then went to bed.

Saturday 2nd January 2016

Dear Yvonne,
Yesterday, I enjoyed a 'easy does it', day. I relaxed, ate. Drank cups of tea, washed my laundry, sent tweets, and posts. I charged my wireless speakers. I charged my GoPro Hero4 Camera and GoPro wireless control via my Windows 10 HP Computer and downloaded the app: Final Cut Pro Plus and GoPro Channel. I used my Logic Pro X app on my Apple MacBook. I updated my Instagram and my 'Care and Concern' blog. Listened to BBC Radio Four and read some of my amazon kindle ebook on my iPhone. I also noticed via my 'OU Anywhere' Open University app on my iPad Air2 that my next module is accessible online. In the evening I went for a short walk to watch the film 'Sherlock Holmes – The Abominable Bride' starring Benedict Cumberbatch, which was Outstanding, in my area at The Ritzy Bar in Brixton, Coldharbour Ward and while at the Ritzy Bar, I bought a ticket for one for this evening, to watch the Transgender film: Danish Girl. I aim to download the app: 'Final Cut Pro X' on to my Apple MacBook. Just for Today, I am preparing to commit to a few hours of Open University studies then to shop for food at Marks & Spencer [M&S] rest. Then watch the film: Danish Girl. Today my beloved son James, sent me a email wishing me a 'Happy New Year. This evening, I spoke with my beloved son James, via Apple FaceTime.

Sunday 3rd January 2016

Dear Yvonne,
I am grateful I downloaded the images from my
Apple GoPro Hero Camera, edited and posted a
'Cycle to Work' film. In addition, I downloaded the
'Man to Woman' Amazon kindle ebook about the
first Sex Change by Lili Elbe, after watching Eddie
Redmayne starring in the film: Danish Girl.

Monday 4th January 2016

Dear Yvonne,
Last night, I ate a delicious M&S Spaghetti
Bolognese and I offered to support Robert Flints
Lambeth and Southwark, London Assembly,
Mayoral Election with some campaigning at The
Oval. After work; I got off the bus in Brixton
Coldharbour Ward and walked home. I put out my
rubbish bin bags for the refuse collectors and
downloaded a Logic Pro X Podcast of '2016 New
Years Resolution' to SoundClouds and listened to
it via my SoundCloud app on my iPhone. I had a
wonderful relaxing scented candlelit bubblebath,
checked and adjusted my online banking and fell
asleep listening to BBC Radio Four. Today, just
had breakfast. Now resting and sipping tea.

Tuesday 4th January 2016

Dear Yvonne,
Just eaten my breakfast, after a restful peaceful
night's sleep, I am now reflecting on my gratitude
for my FaceTime conversation with my beloved

son James and his visit yesterday evening. I am grateful, that yesterday I visited the Apple Store and bought wireless headphones. I have paired it via Bluetooth with my iPhone. In addition, yesterday, I went for a divine cup of English Breakfast Tea, at The Ritzy Bar in Brixton Coldharbour Ward; followed an after work, exquisite bottle of Sparkling Water with lemon and lime slices with ice from my local area Effra Hall pub on the corner of Rattray Road and Kellett Road, Brixton Coldharbour Ward.

Wednesday 6th January 2016

Dear Yvonne,
Today I am on a late shift at work. My beloved son James told me via FaceTime that he is visiting me today before I go to work, for a McDonald's meal. I have just eaten breakfast and am sipping a cup of tea. I have taken my 'Stella' anti-psychotic mental health mental health medication. Just for Today, I aim to spend the morning in an easy does it way, lazing in bed in a Stonewall UK t-shirt and pyjamas, reading a Niall Ferguson book. I have been reading Niall Ferguson for years and years, one day at a time. Today's Niall Ferguson book is 'High Financier – The Lives and Time of Siegmund Warburg. – which is about the banker 'Siegmund Warburg' which I have downloaded on to my Amazon Kindle as well as via Apple iBook on my Apple iPad Air 2, which I started reading last night on my Apple MacBook after briefly scanning the ebook 'Alan Turing' by Andrew Hodges; about the World War Two Homosexual Enigma Code breaker which the film: 'The

Imitation Game' was based on starring the actor Benedict Cumberbatch, which I watched with my beloved son James at The Ritzy Bar.

Thursday 7th January 2016

Dear Yvonne,
I am grateful and happy tomorrow I meet with my Freemason Lodge Adelaide Litten No.23. It will be a practice at the home of W. Bro. Cynthia H Ramsay.

Friday 8th January 2016

Dear Yvonne,
A great time was had by me last night, using various combinations ie watching the film: The Iron Lady; starring Meryl Streep. While Microsoft at the same time being able to access my Twitter tweets; annotation – highlighting editing from PDF Connoisseur Reader while also reading from Amazon App ebook: Kissinger by Niall Ferguson. As well as a variety of other pairings including Excel side by side with Microsoft Word with my split Screen Apple iPad Air 2.

Saturday 9th January 2016

Dear Yvonne,
Yesterday my beloved son James spoke to me via FaceTime and then visited me for a few hours. We dined on a McDonalds meal. In the evening, I went to 27 Pembridge Gardens, Notting Hill Gate, to my Adelaide Litten No.23 Freemason Lodge

Practice, on the bus listening in my headphones to Apple iTunes downloaded 'Mozart for Brain Power' music. On the bus homeward bound to Brixton, via the Houses Of Parliament, I sent an email via my iPhone to my local Quaker Friends Overseers, Clerk and Elder giving my apologies for forthcoming 14th January 2016 Meeting absence, due to 73 Stamford Street Homeless Charity Waterloo work commitments. I then read chapters six and seven of the second book of Samuels, from the King James Bible via my Apple iBooks on my iPhone and then continued to read Kissinger by Niall Ferguson.

Sunday 10th January 2016

Dear Yvonne,
Yesterday I spent a wonderful face to face contact time with my beloved son James. David Bowie, Brixton Boy, who is on record as describing himself as bisexual, died today. RIP.

Monday 11th January 2016,

Dear Yvonne,
Just for Today, my goal is to take an hour to read and study a chapter of my OU-Open University module ebook .Personal Finance. Today I went to Regent Street Apple Store and paid for a iPad Pro, and took it home on the bus and proceeded to make it ready for my use by downloading some of the following apps: Microsoft Word, Excel, Powerpoint, plus Keynote, Pages, Numbers, PDF Connoisseur Reader. Twitter, Kindle.

Tuesday 12th January 2016

Dear Yvonne,
Today I received my OU-Open University module course material in the post. In addition, I paired my Apple Hero Camera to my iPad Pro, using the GoPro app and downloaded the following apps: GarageBand, iMovie. This evening I spoke with my beloved son James via Apple FaceTime and then my son visited me briefly and we dined on McDonalds. I then took a bath and went to bed.

Wednesday 13th January 2016

Dear Yvonne,
Today I downloaded the GoPro app on to my iPhone and used it. Took a few screen shots of the process and posted it on my Care and Concern blog; plus I tweeted it on Tweeter and posted it on FaceBook and Instagram.

Thursday 14th January 2016

Dear Yvonne,
Today my goal is to reply to Stephen, my OU-Open University Personal Finance module tutors email. This evening, I aim to read a bit of my Freemason literature.

Friday 15th January 2016

Dear Yvonne,
Today I enjoyed an exquisite 3rd Degree Ceremony at my Women Only Adelaide Litten

No.23 Freemason Lodge at The Order Of
Women's Freemasons, 27 Pembridge Gardens,
Notting Hill Gate, London UK.

Saturday 16th January 2016

Dear Yvonne,
Today I had a face to face visit from my son.

Sunday 17th January 2016

Dear Yvonne,
Today I am celebrating the first Anniversary of the
marriage of Mr Stephen Fry to his husband Mr
Elliott Spencer.

Monday 18th January 2016

Dear Yvonne,
I completed a list of my available dates for contact
with my Beloved son James following a request
from him to his foster mother. It worked out to be
face to face every other Saturday. With FaceTime
contact on the Saturdays which I don't have face
to face contact. In addition, I have included phone
calls every week. I am waiting to hear from his
foster mother which of my dates have been
accepted,

Tuesday 19th January 2016

Dear Yvonne,
Today my supervisor, who is also the Lead
Manager of my 73 Stamford Street, Waterloo
Project Hostel, told me that she is leaving her job

and has already handed in her notice. I needed some head space to clear my head, so asked for and took half an hour of toil- time of in lieu. I took a 59 bus to Brixton and paid for a cup of English Breakfast Tea at the Ritzy Bar. I then slowly sipped my delicious cup of tea whilst playing a game of computerized Chess on my Tesco Hudl 2 Android Tablet. The computer won.

Wednesday 20th January 2016

Dear Yvonne,
Today I met with Primrose from GP Plus, for the first time. GP Plus is my third sector mental health organisation which has taken me from my Brixton CMHT-Community Mental Health NHS-National Health Service team and liaises with my GP-General Practitioner regarding my mental health. When Primrose came to my door today, we arranged for her to park her vehicle in Tesco's car park and meet me at the Ritzy Bar. I spoke with Primrose for approximately one hour, while sipping a tomato Juice with Wooster sauce. We have arranged to meet again at 15:30hrs on Tuesday 22nd March 2016.

Thursday 21st January 2016

Dear Yvonne,
Today I started a Change.Org Petition. The campaign is for John Bercow MP and Speaker of The House of Commons, Angela Eagle MP, Margot James MP, Helen Hayes MP, Wes Streeting MP, Diane Abbott MP, Chukka Umunna

MP and Kate Hoey MP to create a Commission for Gay Males; and a Committee for Gay Males in the House of Commons.

Friday 22nd January 2016

Dear Yvonne,
Today I washed clothes, did ironing, rested in bed; dozing. Then I showered and did some food shopping at M&S. My beloved son James has just spoken to me via FaceTime and is going to Face to Face visit me briefly within the next hour.

Saturday 23rd January 2016

Dear Yvonne,
Today I am down to my last few pounds sterling cash before I get my salary on Thursday; but at least I have enough food in my fridge to last until then. I had face to face contact with my beloved son James and just managed to scrap together monies for an M&S sandwich for him.

Sunday 24th January 2016

Dear Yvonne.
Had an extra special day today. Introduced someone to CoDa - Co-dependency Anonymous and tuned into a Yoga Meeting via the live video online website 'In the Rooms'. Today is the fifty-first anniversary of Sir Winston Churchill's death. I am grateful to have visited Chartwell and had drinks in the presence of his grandson, Nicholas Soames.

Monday 25th January 2016

Dear Yvonne,
Today my bank informed me via text that I have
insufficient funds to pay my bills. I also received
an email from Time to Change informing me that
the day time television programme facilitators of
'Good Morning Britain' has seen my television
advert with Birgit Rapp and would like to film us
and perhaps we may appear on live on their show
for the 5th February 'Time to Talk' day; with the
filming. Today I also spoke with my son via
FaceTime.

Tuesday 26th January 2016

Dear Yvonne,
Today I had a conversation with my beloved son
James via FaceTime. James then gave me a face
to face visit for a few hours and twenty pounds,
which I spent in M&S.

Wednesday 27th January 2016

Dear Yvonne,
Today I enjoyed a lovely lie-in before going to
work in the afternoon.

Thursday 28th January 2016

Dear Yvonne,
Today at work, I had my last supervision session
with my boss, who is leaving soon. My beloved
son spoke to me via FaceTime and told me that

he is going to give me a face to face visit today; and visited briefly. We shared some McDonald's food.

Friday 29th January 2016

Dear Yvonne,
Today I participated in a Lambeth Money Know How for Social Housing Tenants workshop at St Luke's hub in Kennington. This evening I took part in a live chat on FaceBook as part of the OUSA-Open University Student Association London Region Executive Assembly rep, for the London Area Freshers; and then I was visited in the evening by my beloved son James. We shared some M&S food.

Saturday 30th January 2016

Dear Yvonne,
This morning I spent an hour sipping tea and reading in Costa in Waterstones bookshop in Trafalgar Square.

Sunday 31st January 2016

Dear Yvonne,
This morning, I participated in my local Brixton and Streatham Quaker Friends Meeting for Worship. Today it was a Business Meeting. Afterwards, I went for brunch at the Ritzy Bar and ate toast, scrambled eggs and salmon with a cup of English Breakfast Tea. In addition, I purchased a ticket for this forthcoming Tuesday at 18:10hrs to watch the film: The revenant.

Monday 1st February 2016

Dear Yvonne,
Today I received an invitation from Wes Streeting MP inviting me to attend Ilford North Labour Party's annual dinner with Guardian columnist and best-selling author Owen Jones, as well as other special guests. Though I would love to have spent some time in Wes' company…I declined the invitation. Today I spoke with my beloved son James, via FaceTime. James asked if he could come and meet me at home after I finish work today and did so. We dined on a McDonald's meal.

Tuesday 2nd February 2016

Dear Yvonne,
Today after work, I watched the film: The Revenant. Then I spoke with my beloved son James, via FaceTime. James asked me if he could meet me at home; and did. We dined on M&S

Wednesday 3rd February 2016

Dear Yvonne,
Today before work, I visited the Regent Street Apple Store. My beloved son James spoke to me via FaceTime while I was at work, asking if he could meet me at home. Sadly I said no, because I wasn't going to be home until approximately midnight.

Thursday 4th February 2016

Dear Yvonne,
I had my annual work appraisal, as a Thames
Reach Hostel Support Worker with my manager
today in the Royal Festival Hall. After work I tried
to attend the OUSA-Open University Student
Association London Executive Assembly meet-up
at the Doggett Coats and Badge; sadly I arrived
too late and spent my time there reading my
kindle, while sipping English breakfast tea. This
evening my beloved son James spoke to me via
FaceTime and then visited me. We shared an
M&S meal.

Friday 5th February 2016

Dear Yvonne,
Today I spent most of the day in my Stonewall t-
shirt and pyjamas bottoms. After having breakfast,
I did a bit of OU-Open University module
preparation; in addition to some Order of Women
Freemasonry preparation. This afternoon I
participated in a phone interview for Stonewall
regarding my voluntary role on the Stonewall 25
Workplace from Section 28 to Equal Marriage.
Today I received the formal Agenda and Minutes
for my Tuesday 16th February 2016 Dulwich &
West Norwood Conservative Association. Herne
Hill and Coldharbour Wards Annual General
Meeting. I have held the officer role of Treasurer.
This evening, my beloved son James has just
spoken to me via FaceTime and asked if he can
visit. Of course, I said yes.

Saturday 6th February 2016

Dear Yvonne,
Today is the start of my new OU-Open University
module DB123: You and Your Money: Personal
Finance in Context. I spent the morning studying
on my bed, dressed in my pyjamas. This afternoon
I hosted a OUSA-Open University Student
Association London Executive Assembly meet-up,
at the Ritzy Bar in my local Brixton Coldharbour
Ward. To my knowledge, one person turned up
and I spent an hour and a half in interesting
conversation with him. This evening my spoke on
the phone to my dear old friend Birgit. I had
missed her voice and though her voice was
huskier than usual, due to a recent operation, it
was lovely to speak with her. In addition, my
beloved son James spoke to me via FaceTime
and then visited. We dined on KFC

Sunday 7th February 2016

Dear Yvonne,
Today is the 56th birthday of C, the love of my life
and I have annual leave from work. This morning I
attended a Meeting for Worship at my local Brixton
and Streatham Meeting House. After meeting
today, I took the over ground train to Sutton to
attend a Quaker Elders and Overseers Meeting at
Sutton Quaker Meeting House. I met Antony
Barlow, who has just had his family history 'He is
Our Cousin, Cousin: A Quaker Family History from
1660 to the present…' published and traces his

Quaker ancestors beyond the start of the campaign for the abolition of slavery and William Wilberforce. On my way home from Sutton, I stopped off at my local Effra Hall Pub and sipped bottled sparkling water with ice and sliced lemon and lime; whilst reading 'Kissinger' from my Amazon kindle app on my iPad. In the background I could hear intermittent cheers, as folk watched football on the large television screens in the bar. This evening, I have an online Open University tutorial. Great!

Monday 8th February 2016

Dear Yvonne,
Today I spent several hours in Broadstairs Kent, attending a Meeting, on work related business for my 73 Stamford Street Waterloo Thames Reach Homelessness Charity. I spoke to my beloved son James via FaceTime, when I arrived home.

Tuesday 9th February 2016

Dear Yvonne,
The sea air must have knocked me out last night. It was so hard to wake for my early shift this morning. I spoke to my beloved son James via FaceTime and he visited me today. We dined on M&S and KFC.

Wednesday 10th February 2016

Dear Yvonne,
Today I have an annual day leave from work and spent most of it sleeping. I spoke with my beloved

son via FaceTime and he is going to visit me.
Today we ate birthday cake.

Thursday 11th February 2016

Dear Yvonne,
Today back at work. Officially spoke with the new
manager of the hostel. Spoke with my beloved son
James via FaceTime and was briefly visited by
him.

Friday 12th February 2016

Dear Yvonne,
Met with my lawyer today and visited my bank.
Then I went to the Ritzy Bar and read part of a
book on my Amazon Kindle app from my iPad;
while sipping English Breakfast tea. I spoke with
my beloved son James via FaceTime. James is
going to respite from his foster placement today
until Tuesday. This evening I took a long hot
bubble bath while listening to Absolute Radio
Classic Rock. I followed my bath by using my iPad
to draw while continuing to listen to rock music. I
ended the evening reading some of the William
Shakespeare play 'A Midsummer Night's Dream'
by the RSC – Royal Shakespeare Company and
listening to Tchaikovsky.

Saturday 13th February 2016

Dear Yvonne,
Today is the day of my late mother's birth. I
attended a OU-Open University Day School

Tutorial at the LSE – London School of Economics. This afternoon, I stopped off for a bottled Sparling Water with slices of lemon and lime with ice at my local Effra Hall pub and read a bit of Shakespeare from my Amazon kindle while there. In the evening, I attended a QLGF – Quaker Lesbian & Gay Fellowship at the Westminster Friends Meeting House.

Sunday 14th February 2016

Dear Yvonne,
Today is Valentine's Day. My beloved son James is away at Respite and C, the love of my life is currently in Moscow. I am especially glad to be working at the Hostel today.

Monday 15th February 2016

Dear Yvonne,
Today I took one day's annual leave off from work. I had a lie-in this morning, then shopped for food at M&S and spent some time this afternoon sipping tea and studying in the Ritzy Bar. This evening, I spent approximately one hour in my local Brixton Coldharbour Ward, Effra Hall Pub.

Tuesday 16th February 2016

Dear Yvonne,
Today was a work day. It seemed especially cold, though dry. This evening, I attended a Dulwich and West Norwood Conservative Association, Herne Hill and Coldharbour Wards AGM - Annual General Meeting. This evening, I gave my

apologies in advance for being unable to attend Thursday 18th February 2016 Dulwich and West Norwood Executive Council Meeting, due to work commitments.

Wednesday 17th February 2016

Dear Yvonne,
Today I felt especially tired and had a lie in before going to work for my late shift. My beloved son James spoke to me via FaceTime while I was at work and again when I got home close to midnight. James wanted to see me face to face today before he goes away again for a week tomorrow. I agreed that he could see me briefly tomorrow morning before I leave for work at approximately 9am. James told me he would call by tomorrow at 7am.

Thursday 18th February 2016

Dear Yvonne,
Today I rang James, just after 8am to find out if he was on his way; but I got no answer. I left for work at 09:30am. This evening I arrived home from work at 21:30pm. Shattered.

Friday 19th February 2016

Dear Yvonne,
Today was my day off. I slept for most of the morning and then I visited my Lawyer again. In the evening, I spoke to a few friends on the phone and had an early night.

Saturday 20th February 2016

Dear Yvonne,
Today I had an OU-Open University Day School at the LSE-London School of Economics. Outstanding. In the evening, I visited Peckham to see friends. Sadly one of them is not too well at the moment. Mental Health issues.

Sunday 21st February 2016

Dear Yvonne,
Today I missed Quaker meeting as I was very tired and spent all morning sleeping. This afternoon I went to work. My beloved son James, spoke to me via FaceTime and told me that he has returned from his break. We have arranged to see each other face to face tomorrow evening, after I finish work.

Monday 22nd February 2016

Dear Yvonne,
I spent most of this morning sleeping. I received a phone call, this afternoon while at work from my son's foster carers supervisor inviting me to a

meeting for my son today. I rang her back and was told that the meeting was currently taking place and the next meeting will be at my son's foster placement at 16:00hrs on 13th April 2016. This evening, after work, I spoke to my son via FaceTime, then met face to face with my beloved son James and he told me that the meeting went well. I asked my son about his education, and he told me that he will be starting to attend The Princes' Trust within three weeks. I am pleased. Very pleased.

Tuesday 23rd February 2016

Dear Yvonne,
This morning I started work at 07:00hrs. I am feeling very tired. This evening my beloved son James spoke to me via FaceTime and then visited me.

Wednesday 24th February 2016

Dear Yvonne,
Today was annual leave. This morning I attended the first of four weeks of four hour weekly sessions of Bike Maintenance Course at the Ace Of Clubs Day Centre, run by Cycle Training UK. Wow, I didn't know that Brompton Bikes were so complex.

Thursday 25th February 2016
Today, I spent most of the morning sleeping on and off and listening to Radio Four and Absolute Radio Rock on digital. After work this evening my beloved son James spoke to me via FaceTime and then visited me Face to Face.

Friday 26th February 2016

Dear Yvonne,
Today was my day off. I went to International House in Brixton to try to find the social worker of my beloved son James. I finally located him in Streatham, in a building behind the cinema. We spoke for some time. I gave him seventy pounds to pay for a bike maintenance course for my beloved son James and I also gave him a application form for him to send off for a provisional driving licence for my beloved son James so that I can book lessons for my son and ensure that he has his first driving lesson on his seventeenth birthday. This evening my beloved son James spoke to me via FaceTime and then he visited me Face To Face.

Saturday 27th February 2016

Dear Yvonne,
Today I spent the day at the OU-Open University in Camden attending Consultation. This evening I had Face to Face contact with my beloved son James.

Sunday 28th February 2016

Dear Yvonne,
I spent this morning in bed sleeping. This afternoon I went to work.

Monday 29th February 2016

Dear Yvonne,
Today, Leap Day, I started work at 07:00hrs. Today my beloved son James spoke to me via FaceTime and then visited me Face to Face this evening. I worked on my soon to be submitted TMA-Tutor Marked Assessment.

Tuesday 1st March 2016

Dear Yvonne,
Today I started work at 07:00hrs. Today I took 'Jet' the Waterloo Project cat to the vets. When I came home I spoke to my beloved son James via FaceTime and he came to visit me Face to Face this evening. I continued working on my Tutor Marked Assessment. After my son left for the night, I submitted my online assessment to be marked by my tutor.

Wednesday 2nd March 2016

Dear Yvonne,
This morning I spent four hours at the Ace of Club Day Centre, attending my Bike Maintenance Course. This was week two of the four week

course. It's great! This is the second week that I have cycled to the course and back on my Brompton Bike. However I took the bus to work this afternoon.

Thursday 3rd March 2016

Dear Yvonne,
Today I had an annual leave day off from work. I spent most of the day sleeping. This afternoon I took a bus to Euston Station and purchased a return train ticket for my forthcoming Saturday trip to Milton Keynes. My son spoke with me via FaceTime and visited me Face to Face this evening.

Friday 4th March 2016

Dear Yvonne,
Today was my day off from my Waterloo Homeless Charity. I spent most of the day in bed. I slept on and off for about twelve hours. This afternoon, I showered and went to The Ritzy Bar for a cup of English Breakfast Tea and a pizza. Then I took buses to Notting Hill Gate to attend my Freemason Lodge.

Saturday 5th March 2016

Dear Yvonne,
Today I spent the day in Milton Keynes to attend the OUSA-Open University Student Association Regional and National Representatives' Seminar. The Theme was: Moving Forward Together. It was the first time I have ever visited Milton Keynes. My

beloved son James, spoke to me via FaceTime while I was in Milton Keynes and gave me a Face to Face visit on my return to London, this evening. Today I received my mark from my Tutor Marked assessment. Room for improvement.

Sunday 6th March 2016

Dear Yvonne,
Today is Mothers' Day. I spent the morning sleeping in bed and then went to work. I did not hear from my beloved son James today. I am sad and disappointed.

Monday 7th March 2016

Dear Yvonne,
I spent the morning sleeping in bed and went to work in the afternoon. Today is the start of my new work rota. My beloved son James spoke to me today at 18:00hrs via FaceTime and wished me a Happy Mothers Day.

Tuesday 8th March 2016

Dear Yvonne.
Today is International Women's Day. I have taken annual leave. I feel fatigued. Spent all morning sleeping in bed and got up at around 15:00hrs. Went to M&S and Sainsbury's to purchase Appletise and Mint Imperials for my beloved son James. This afternoon I spent sipping English

Breakfast tea and eating a Vegan Salad in The Ritzy Bar in Brixton. I purchased a ticket to watch a Saturday 23rd April 2016, two hour Shakespeare live screening performance by Sir Ian McKellen, Judi Dench… to celebrate William Shakespeare's 400th Anniversary My beloved son James spoke to me via FaceTime. He said that he will Face to Face visit me after my meeting and he did. This evening I attended the Dulwich & West Norwood Conservative Association Annual General Meeting in Dulwich. I was pleased to see everyone, including Robert Flint, and continued enlisting support to be the first Black Openly Lesbian Member of Parliament to take my seat for Dulwich & West Norwood Conservative Association at the 2020 General Election.

Wednesday 9th March 2016

Dear Yvonne,
This morning I attended the third session of my Bike Maintenance course at The Ace of Clubs Day Centre, with the Cycle Training UK tutor. Afterwards, I dined on a Pizza in Brixton Market at Franco Manca. I then visited my solicitor. Today I received a phone call from SANE; asking if I would like to do a Mental Health interview and photo shoot for The SUN newspaper; and told me that they will be able to tell me more tomorrow morning. I said I would be interested. I sent a text to my dear old friend Birgit Rapp to inform her. Birgit replied that it will be great exposure, as long as it isn't 'Page 3' This evening I wanted to watch the live screening from the ENO-English National Opera of Mozart's 'The Magic Flute' at my local

Ritzy Cinema this evening; but it was cancelled. I can get a refund but I am disappointed. I have now booked a ticket to see 'The Magic Flute' live at the London Coliseum at 3pm on Saturday 19th March 2016. This evening my beloved son James spoke to me via FaceTime and asked if he could visit me this evening. I said yes, and we have been dining on M&S food.

Thursday 10th March 2016

Dear Yvonne,
Another annual leave day. Received a phone call from SANE today to say I am not needed for the Mental Health interview by The SUN. I am disappointed. I spent this evening looking at photos of my late mother, my beloved son James and myself. My beloved son James spoke with me via FaceTime.

Friday 11th March 2016

Dear Yvonne,
Today is my day off. I relaxed for most of the day. This evening, I started contacting public places for me to facilitate a future online EU Referendum for folks in Brixton and surrounding areas to be able to be presented with both sides of the debate, to aide them when they vote. The EU Referendum online Tool is the brainchild of the ERS-Electoral Reform Society.

Saturday 12th March 2016

Dear Yvonne,
Today is my day off. It is also my Face to Face
Contact day with my beloved son James. We
dined on a delivered Domino Pizza. The Pizza
reminded me of my mother. She learned how to
make pizza specially for my son James. This
evening, my cousin Joe rang me from Jamaica.
Joe is my late mother's second eldest brother's
son.

Sunday 13th March 2016

Dear Yvonne,
After a lovely lie-in this morning, I was back at
work this afternoon. I informed my Thames Reach
Lead Manager, her Lambeth Area Manager and
the Chief Executive - Mr Jeremy Swain of my
intentions to be the first Black openly lesbian
Conservative MP to be seated at the 2020
General Election. Today I am delighted that
@LGBToryUK and @ElectoralReform are now
amongst my amazing twitter followers.

Monday 14th March 2016

Dear Yvonne,
This morning before work, I visited the Brixton
Soup Kitchen and the Beehive Pub regarding
facilitating a possible EU Referendum event. I
then stopped off for lunch at The Ritzy Bar. Whilst
at work this afternoon, I found that my Thames
Reach Chief Executive - Mr Jeremy Swain had

sent an email stating his admiration for my determination - aside from political differences. I also received a phone call from the Karibu Education Centre, in Brixton and to confirm that they would be okay about me facilitating a EU Referendum event in their conference room. Today I spoke to my beloved son James via FaceTime.

Tuesday 15th March 2016

Dear Yvonne,
Yesterday I signed up to do a 5K walk in Crystal Palace on the 12th June 2016 for Cancer Research UK. I am hoping to raise a minimum five thousand pounds for this cause using the http://www.justgiving.com/yvonnestewart-williams I have donated the first thirty pounds, and posted it on Facebook and Twitter. Today I visited Brixton Soup Kitchen in Coldharbour Ward Brixton, where I had a cup of tea and met Solomon Smith, who gave me a tour of the premises. I will officially start volunteering for Brixton Soup Kitchen from next Monday 21st March 2016 at 11am. Today I spoke with my beloved son James via FaceTime. James has told me that he is going to visit me Face to Face tomorrow. Today I have agreed to participate in a Dulwich and West Norwood Conservatives Association Action Day this Saturday 19th March 2016 from 10am until approximately 1pm.

Wednesday 16th March 2016

Dear Yvonne,
Today I had a day's annual leave from work and I attended my fourth and final Bike Maintenance course with Cycle Training UK at the Ace of Clubs Day Centre in Clapham. It was a fantastic course and has inspired me to think about enrolling on a Day Brompton Cycle Maintenance Course run by Cycle Training UK in Bermondsey on Saturday 11th June 2016. Today was the Budget. It was delivered by my Conservative colleague George Osborne MP, his eighth. This afternoon my beloved son James gave me a Face to Face visit. We dined on Domino's pizza. My son saved me the last slice of pizza. Aw bless!

Thursday 17th March 2016

Dear Yvonne,
Today I started work at 7am and had Supervision with my new Lead Manager. My beloved son spoke to me via FaceTime and came to visit me at home after I finished work. We dined on Domino Pizza.

Friday 18th March 2016

Dear Yvonne,
Today was my day off. I spent it sleeping in bed and listening to BBC Radio Four. This evening I attended my Order of Women's Freemasonry, Lodge Adelaide Litten No.23

Saturday 19th March 2016

Dear Yvonne,
Today was my day off. I spent the morning in
Dulwich on a DWNCA - Dulwich & West Norwood
Conservative Association Action Day in support of
the Mayoral candidate Zac Goldsmith and
Lambeth & Southwark London Assembly
candidate Robert Flint. This afternoon I visited the
London Coliseum to watch the Mozart Opera 'The
Magic Flute', performed by the ENO - English
National Opera. Marvellous! This evening my
beloved son James spoke to me via FaceTime
and then visited me Face to Face. We dined on
McDonalds and M&S food and drink.

Sunday 20th March 2016

Dear Yvonne,
Today is the first day of Spring. It is also my
annual leave day off. I was on Welcoming duties
at my local Brixton & Streatham Quaker Friends
House, Meeting for Worship today. I enjoyed a
serene meeting and was grateful that I managed
to rise from my bed on time, though I felt sluggish
and tired this morning.

Monday 21st March 2016

Dear Yvonne,
Today was the first of my two days of annual leave
day off this week. This morning I had a short lie-in
before visiting my bank and then starting my first

day at 11am as a volunteer at the Brixton Soup
Kitchen on Coldharbour lane. Time really flew and
before I knew it, it was 2pm and time to leave.
This evening I spent two hours at CCHQ-
Conservative Campaign HeadQuarters
participating in Phone Canvas volunteering in
favour of Zac Goldsmith.

Tuesday 22nd March 2016

Dear Yvonne,
Today I spent the whole morning snoozing on and
off while listening to the radio. This afternoon I met
with Primrose, my Third Sector Mental Health
Community Psychiatric Nurse at the Ritzy Bar. I
arrived a little late for Primrose, due to stopping on
the way for a chat with Mrs Mills, a 90 year old
Coldharbour Ward neighbour; who I normally see
standing at her front gate with her cat named 'Cat',
within sight. Today time with Primrose flew
especially after she revealed that her sister is gay
and married to a woman. Primrose told me that
there are family members who her sister is now
estranged from. As Primrose is Black African, I
anticipated that. However Primrose's family much
like my own found that Gay issues became
normalised due to being of a personal nature. This
evening at 17:30hrs, a Labour Party activist rang
my door bell and asked if I would be voting for
Sadiq Khan on the 5th May 2016. What do you
think? I spoke with my beloved son James via
FaceTime and James gave me a Face to Face
visit this evening.

Wednesday 23rd March 2016

Dear Yvonne,
Today after work, my beloved son James spoke with me via FaceTime and then gave me a Face to Face visit.

Thursday 24th March 2016

Dear Yvonne,
Today I continued the internal process with my Political Party of trying to realise my dream of being the first Black openly lesbian Conservative MP at the 2020 General Election.

Friday 25th March 2016

Dear Yvonne,
Today is Good Friday and I spent my day off sleeping and listening to BBC Radio Four.

Saturday 26th March 2016

Dear Yvonne,
Today is my day off and I spent the morning in College Ward, Canvassing for Zac Goldsmith, Robert Flint and Kate Bramson with my Dulwich and West Norwood Conservative Association after stopping off for a Cup of tea and chat at the Allen Head Pub, I spoke to my beloved son via FaceTime and arranged to meet him as planned at my place. This afternoon my beloved son James and I sat chatting, eating, listening to Radio Absolute Rock and using IT.

Sunday 27th March 2016

Dear Yvonne,

Today is Easter Sunday and the clocks were put forward one hour in the early hours of this morning. It is also my annual leave day off from work. I spent most of the morning sleeping, so missed my Quaker Friends Meeting for Worship, but I at least attended a Overseers, Elder and Clerk meeting at my local Brixton & Streatham Quaker Friends Meeting House. This evening my beloved son James spoke with me via FaceTime.

Monday 28th March 2016

Dear Yvonne,
Today is Bank Holiday Monday and my annual day off from work. I spent most of the day in doors and doing laundry, and Open University homework. This evening my beloved son James spoke to my via FaceTime and then gave me a Face to Face visit.

Tuesday 29th March 2016

Dear Yvonne,
Today is the second anniversary of the first day that Equal Same Sex Marriage in England and Wales could legally take place. It is my annual day off from work. I spent the morning volunteering at the Brixton Soup Kitchen. This afternoon I visited the Karibu Education Centre at 7 Gresham Road, Brixton SW9 and booked a three hour slot for 18:30-21:30hrs on Tuesday 21st February 2017

for the Coldharbour & Herne Hill Wards
Conservative Branch AGM-Annual General
Meeting. I followed this with stopping off at the
Ritzy Bar, in Brixton for a delicious cup of Earl
Gray tea. This evening I did a spot of Order of
Women's Freemasonry revision and spoke to my
beloved son Jame via FaceTime. James then
gave me a Face to Face visit.

Wednesday 30th March 2016

Dear Yvonne,
Today is my annual day off from work. I spent the
morning at the Ace of Club Day Centre in
Clapham part facilitating a Bike Maintenance
Drop-in. This afternoon, I spent time with my
Thames Reach Waterloo Project Homelessness
Charity team, colleagues playing Bowling at the
Elephant & Castle Bowling Alley; for a belated
2015 Xmas event. When I arrived home this
evening, my beloved son spoke to me via
FaceTime and then gave me a Face to Face visit.

Thursday 31st March 2016

Dear Yvonne,
Today is my annual leave day off from work. I had
a lie-in and then visited my bank and my solicitor
and then did some M&S shopping for perishable
foods. This evening, I attended a Brixton
Neighbourhood Forum meeting at the Vida Walsh
Centre.

Friday 1st April 2016

Dear Yvonne,
Today is my day off. I had a lie in and then went
shopping for a few bits in my local PC World
Curry's and then had lunch in The Ritzy Bar. My
son spoke with me via FaceTime and then came
to visit me. I ordered food via Deliveroo.

Saturday 2nd April 2016

Dear Yvonne,
This morning I was with my DWNCA members in
Dulwich & Herne Hill dressed in my 'Nobody know
I'm a Lesbian' tee-shirt, I was speechless for the
peaceful protesters in the Carnegie Library. This
afternoon I delivered Zac Goldsmith & Robert Flint
leaflets in Coldharbour Ward. This evening I
watched the Met Madame Butterfly Opera, live at
the Ritzy Cinema.

Sunday 3rd April 2016

Dear Yvonne,
This morning I was on Welcoming duties at my
local Brixton & Streatham Quaker Friends Meeting
for Worship. I stopped off for a scrambled eggs,
salmon, toast and Earl Gray tea brunch; in the
Ritzy Bar. I did a bit of OU studies and then I went
back to my Thames Reach Homelessness
Charity.

Monday 4th April 2016

Dear Yvonne,
This morning I volunteered at the Brixton Soup
Kitchen and visited Stonewall then went to work
for a Late Shift.

Tuesday 5th April 2016

Dear Yvonne,
This morning I arrived at work at approximately
09:30hrs to take Jet the cat to be neutered, but Jet
couldn't go to have surgery today as he had eaten
food. I then did my M&S weekly food shop. This
afternoon I was on a late.

Wednesday 6th April 2016

Dear Yvonne,
This morning I volunteered as a Co-facilitator of
the Bike Maintenance Drop-in at the Ace of Clubs
day centre in Clapham. I stopped off for lunch in
The Ritzy Bar, then went for an afternoon sleep.
This evening I attended a LGBTory Candidates'
fundraiser. On my return home I spoke with my
beloved son James. James then gave me a Face
to Face visit.

Thursday 7th April 2016

Dear Yvonne,
This morning I felt very tired. I stopped off for a
takeaway Earl Gray tea at the Ritzy Bar, before
going to work at my Thames Reach Waterloo

Homelessness Charity. Today I received a email confirmation for me to attend the forthcoming Wednesday 13th April 2016 Stonewall and Regard, Equality for LGBT people (with disabilities) - Out for Change event, which is taking place at the Coin Street Neighbourhood Centre. This evening, I had a lovely hot candlelit bubble bath. My beloved son James spoke to me via FaceTime and then gave me a Face to Face visit.

Friday 8th April 2016

Dear Yvonne,
Today was my day off and I spent most of the morning sleeping in bed. I did my laundry and housework and stopped off at the Ritzy Bar for a snack and Earl Gray tea. While in the Ritzy Bar I got on with a bit of OU-Open University studies. This afternoon my beloved son James spoke to me via FaceTime and then visited me with his Social Worker. James' Social Worker reminded me that I am expected at a LAC-Looked After Children Review on Wednesday 13th April 2016, then left ,leaving James with me. This evening I delivered a few more Zac Goldsmith and Robert Flint leaflets locally. Then sent a RSVP request for two forthcoming DWNCA-Dulwich & West Norwood Conservatives Association Social Events with Guest speaker Cllr Tim Briggs, Leader of the Conservative Group, Lambeth Council on Saturday 7th May 2016 and Mrs Kemi Badenoch, DWNCA Parliamentary Candidate in 2010 Now London wide member of the GLA-Greater London Assembly on Saturday 25th June 2016.

Saturday 9th April 2016

Dear Yvonne,
This morning I was on a 08:04hr train heading
towards Worthing and leaving from London
Victoria. I spent the day at the Pembridge Society,
Porchway House Women's Freemason Seminar.
Today I booked to watch a Comedy Freemason
Play in on Saturday 28th May 2016 in Portsmouth.
in On my return to London I spoke with my
beloved son James via FaceTime and then James
gave me a Face to Face visit.

Sunday 10th April 2015

Dear Yvonne,
This morning, I had a long lie-in before going to
work at my full-time Thames Reach Waterloo
Project Homelessness Charity.

Monday 11th April 2015

Dear Yvonne,
This morning before going to work, I volunteered
at the Brixton Soup Kitchen. This evening my
beloved son James spoke to me via FaceTime.

Tuesday 12th April 2016

Dear Yvonne,
This morning before going to work, I went food
shopping in my local Brixton M&S. I was also

given a Face to Face visit by my beloved son James.

Wednesday 13th April 2016

Dear Yvonne,
Today is my annual leave. I spent most of the day at Coin Street Neighbourhood Offices attending a Stonewall and Regard Out for a Change LGBT & Disability event. I left an hour before the end to attend my beloved son James' LAC - Lambeth Looked After Children's Review. However on arrived I found it had been cancelled because I had told James' Social Worker that I was not attending. After a cup of tea and a chat with James' foster mother and supervisor, plus briefly seeing my son James; which was a bonus. I left and went to the LSE - London School of Economics to attend my OU - Open University Tutorial.

Thursday 14th April 2016

Dear Yvonne,
Today I was back at work and working a Client Specialism Day. I finished work for the day at about 18:30hrs and went straight to West Norwood to attend a Dulwich & West Norwood Conservative Association Executive Meeting. After the meeting I had a Face to Face visit from my beloved son James.

Friday 15th April 2016

Dear Yvonne,
Today is my day off. I spent the morning in bed.
Then met up with my dear friend Birgit Rapp in
Starbucks in Vauxhall for a cup of tea and a chat.
This was the first time I had seen Birgit in person
this year! I then spent some time in The Ritzy Bar
and finally was given a Face to Face visit from my
beloved son James on my arrival home, while I
washed my laundry.

Saturday 16th April 2016

Dear Yvonne,
Today I was overcome with hay fever and spent
the whole day sleeping on and off and listening to
the radio.

Sunday 17th April 2016

Dear Yvonne,
This morning I rested in bed and later went to
work at my Thames Reach Waterloo
Homelessness Charity. My beloved son James
spoke to me via FaceTime today.

Monday18th April 2016

Dear Yvonne,
This morning I faceTimed my son at his request
for 8am. He did not reply. Today I felt too tired to
volunteer at Brixton Soup Kitchen and spent the
morning in bed before going to work in the

afternoon. On the way to work, I bumped into my son's foster mother on the underground. This is something which rarely happens. Quite naturally we spoke about James. This evening James spoke with me via FaceTime and asked me to FaceTime him at 8am.

Tuesday 19th April 2016

Dear Yvonne,
This morning I FaceTimed my beloved son James at 8am. He did not reply. This afternoon I set off to work. This evening my beloved son spoke to me via FaceTime. James has asked me to wake him at 8am tomorrow morning via FaceTime.

Wednesday 20th April 2016

Dear Yvonne,
This morning I spoke to my beloved son James via FaceTime at 8am. I was still fatigued with hay-fever and didn't rise from my bed until 10am. I then visited the Ace of Club Day Centre before going to work. Today I purchased and consumed some anti-histamine for my hay-fever. I feel a bit better.

Thursday 21st April 2016

Dear Yvonne,
Today is the 90th birthday of Her Majesty Queen Elizabeth II. I wore my GAP sweatshirt with the union jack on it to work. On my arrival home this

evening, I found I ol;g.nsu80had received my postal ballet in the post for the forthcoming May 5th Mayoral and Greater London Assembly Elections. I completed my forms and posted them this evening. Then I had a lovely soak in a hot candlelit bubble bath.

Friday 22nd April 2016

Dear Yvonne,
This morning I spent my time volunteering for the OU-Open University at the Barbican Centre. I started off by supporting the sales of merchandise and then dressing in a undergraduate gown and leading the staff procession for the Graduate Ceremony and sitting on the stage with the other OU staff and new PhD graduates. The ceremony was amazing. All I have to do now is pass my degrees. Today I listened live via LBC Radio to Prime Minister David Cameron and President Obama, who has been a President for seven years and will leave his post this November were speaking from the Foreign Office on this the last visit of the President to the UK. Barak Obama last visited two years ago and spoke from Westminster. He has visited about five or six times. Today He gave his support to the 'Remain' camp of the EU Referendum, of which David Cameron, who has been a Prime Minister for six years and myself agree; but said ultimately it is for the British Public to decide - on June 23rd 2016. This evening I spoke with my beloved son James via FaceTime. James came to visit me face to face this evening.

Saturday 23rd April 2016

Dear Yvonne,
This morning I was late for my LSE-London School of Economics OU-Open University tutorial, due to being drowsy and pressing the snooze button too often. However my tutorial was fantastic, as always. After tutorial I FaceTimed my beloved son James so that he would know I was on my way home and give me a official pre-arranged Face to Face Contact visit this afternoon. Today is St George's Day and the 400th anniversary of the bard's death. William Shakespeare. This evening I am going to watch a live screening of Shakespeare works at the Ritzy Cinema. James has declined to accompany me.

Sunday 24th April 2016

Dear Yvonne,
My beloved son James spoke to me via FaceTime, just after mid-night this morning, to say that he had left his headphone at my place by mistake. This afternoon, I posted them through his letterbox, whilst making my way to work.

Monday 25th April 2016

Dear Yvonne,
My beloved son James spoke to me via FaceTime this at 02:25hrs this morning; wanting to see me before I go to work. I woke up tired and arrived at the Brixton Soup Kitchen at 11:00hrs to volunteer

before leaving to meet my beloved son James at my home and then leaving for work.

Tuesday 26th April 2016

Dear Yvonne,
Last night I slept for over twelve hours. Today I was on a late shift at my Waterloo workplace. This evening, my beloved son James spoke to me via FaceTime. Afterwork on the bus home I bumped into the very lovely Labour Cllr Jacqui Dyer of Vassell Ward. We greeted each other with a hug and a kiss on the cheeks. Jacqui was with one of her political colleagues and she told me they had just been to a cross borough Scrutiny Health Meeting which started at 18:00 and finished at 22:00hrs. I told Jacqui that I had recently heard her being interviewed on Women's Hour on BBC Radio Four. As Jacqui was getting off the bus, she told me to email her so that we can meet for a coffee.

Wednesday 27th April 2016

Dear Yvonne,
Today I I was on a Mid-Shift at work. Today my beloved son James unsuccessfully tried to call me via FaceTime while I was in a meeting. Later James spoke to me via FaceTime and arranged to meet me Face to Face this evening after work at home; and visited.

Thursday 28th April 2016

Dear Yvonne,
Today my beloved son James spoke with me several times via FaceTime and gave me a brief face to face visit at my home after I finished work for the day. This evening I watched the film Richard III starring Sir Ian McKellen and watched his live satellite interview at The Ritzy Cinema.

Friday 29th April 2016

Dear Yvonne,
This morning, I was so tired that I slept. This afternoon, I went for lunch with Birgit Rapp at the Bonnington Cafe in Vauxhall. It was Birgit's treat and the second time this year that I have seen Birgit. After lunch I visited my bank and then went to see my solicitor and pay my bills. This evening my son spoke to me via FaceTime and then gave me a face to face visit.

Saturday 30th April 2016

Dear Yvonne,
This morning I spent sleeping in bed. I then went for brunch at Ritzy Bar. from 15:00 I spent five hours delivering Robert Flint leaflets in my Coldharbour Ward, where I met a man who in short informed me that he thinks that he cant get involved in Politics because he has been in prison because he had murdered two people. This evening I finally spent doing some OU-Open University studies at home in the company of my beloved son James.

Sunday 1st May 2016

Dear Yvonne,
This morning I did Tea duties at my local Brixton
and Streatham Quaker Meeting for Worship. This
afternoon I visited a sick Quaker inpatient at St
Thomas' Hospital in my capacity of Overseer; then
I went to work at my Thames Reach Waterloo
Homelessness Charity.

Monday 2nd May 2016

Dear Yvonne,
Today is a bank holiday. It is also a work day for
me at the Hostel. Today I submitted a Online
Open University Tutor Marked Assignment to be
checked. Today I spoke with my beloved son
James via FaceTime.

Tuesday 3rd May 2016

Dear Yvonne,
Today I slept all morning, then went to work.

Wednesday 4th May 2016

Dear Yvonne,
Today I went to work for half of the day. This
evening I spoke to my son via FaceTime and then
was visited by him. I attended a urgent Dulwich
and West Norwood Conservative Executive
Council Meeting.

Thursday 5th May 2016

Dear Yvonne,
Today it is Polling Election Day. I started work at
7am. After work I went to sleep for two hours and
then went to the Dulwich & West Norwood
Conservative Election Day Committee Room in
Half Moon Lane, to rustle up some last minute
support for Robert Flint and Zac Goldsmith until
the close of the polling stations.

Friday 6th May 2016

Dear Yvonne,
Day off. Shattered. Phoned and spoke with Birgit
Rapp and also had a conversation via FaceTime
with my beloved son James and then I had a face
to face visit from my son. Zac Goldsmith lost.
Sadiq Khan has become the first Muslim Mayor of
London who was bought up in a Council House
and the son of a Pakistan London bus driving
migrant father. Robert Flint came second.

Saturday 7th May 2016

Dear Yvonne,
I felt exhausted today. Almost overcome with hay
fever. My beloved son James spoke to me via
FaceTime in the night. This evening I briefly spent
time with members of my Dulwich & West
Norwood Conservatives.

Sunday 8th May 2016

Dear Yvonne,
Today is my annual leave day off. Last night my
beloved son James spoke with me via FaceTime
in the night and again this morning. I felt so tired
that I chose to sleep instead of getting up and
visiting Brighton to do the Stonewall Equality
Walk. This afternoon I spoke to a work colleague
on the phone. I then went to the Ritzy Bar for a
cup of Earl Grey tea and phoned and spoke with
my dear friend Brigit Rapp. Today I received good
news via email from Robert Flint to say that we
'Lambeth & Southwark' were one of the few
London boroughs to have had a slight swing from
Labour to the Conservatives and that 'Lambeth &
Southwark' gained its highest figures ever! Bad
news, I received the result of my latest submitted
online assessment. I failed.

Monday 9th May 2016

Dear Yvonne,
Today was a work day. I spent the morning
sleeping.

Tuesday 10th May 2016

Dear Yvonne,
This morning, I volunteered at the Brixton Soup
Kitchen and went to work this afternoon. I spoke
with my son today via FaceTime. Had a lovely
candlelit bubble bath this evening.

Wednesday 11th May 2016

Dear Yvonne,
Today was a work day. I had a cup of Earl Grey tea in the Ritzy Bar beforehand. This afternoon, my beloved son James spoke to me via FaceTime. This evening I was given a face to face visit by my beloved son.

Thursday 12th May 2016

Dear Yvonne,
Today I was at work. It was the last work day for this week. I felt so tired this morning and pressed my alarm snooze button several time before getting out of bed. Today my beloved son James spoke with me via FaceTime. This evening a my son gave me a face to face visit.

Friday 13th May 2016

Dear Yvonne,
Today was my day off. This morning I attended the funeral of my Conservative colleague Dr Enid May Parker 18th April 1920 - 8th April 2016. This afternoon I had lunch with a few of my Conservative WAG's - Women Action Group. This evening I spent my time at my Order of Women Freemasonry Lodge Adelaide Litten No.23. On my return home, I spoke with my beloved son James via FaceTime and then he gave me a face to face visit.

Saturday 14th May 2016

Dear Yvonne,
Today was my day off. I spent the morning sleeping. This afternoon I did a phone interview for SANE to be published in time for Mental Health Awareness Week. This evening, I spoke to my son via FaceTime and was then given a face to face visit.

Sunday 15th May 2016

Dear Yvonne,
I slept all morning and went to work this afternoon.

Monday 16th May 2016

Dear Yvonne,
This morning I overslept and went to volunteer at the Brixton Soup Kitchen via The Ace of Clubs day centre. This afternoon I went to work.

Tuesday 17th May 2016

Dear Yvonne,
Last night my son spoke with me via FaceTime. Then I met with my beloved son before I went to work today. Today SANE published my interview 'Mental Health Issues could lead to a future more enhanced than your past.'

Wednesday 18th May 2016

Dear Yvonne,
Last night my son spoke with me via FaceTime.
Today I spent a day training at Yamyang Buddhist
Centre in Kennington with my Thames Reach
colleagues taught by SLAM - South London and
Maudsley Hospital NHS Trust Psychologists.
Today my SANE interview 'Mental Health Issues
could lead to a future more enhanced than your
past.' was published by the Huffington Post. This
evening I spoke to my son via FaceTime and was
given a face to face visit by him.

Thursday 19th May 2016

Dear Yvonne,
Today I started work at 7am. After work I met with
my dear friend Birgit Rapp for lunch at the Falafel
restaurant in Camberwell. This was Birgit's treat to
me. After lunch we took a bus to Vauxhall and
continued chatting in Starbucks; before finally
attending a Stonewall film event which took place
in the Channel Four building - my treat for Birgit.
We watched the film: Freeheld. On my way home
from the screening, I stopped off in M&S and then
met face to face with my son in my home.

Friday 20th May 2016

Dear Yvonne,

Today is my day off. I spent the morning sleeping
and then met with my solicitor. This evening I

spent time in Notting Hill at my Lodge Adelaide Litten No.23

Saturday 21st May 2016

Dear Yvonne,
This morning I supported the Gypsy Hill by-election campaign. This afternoon I had face to face contact with my beloved son James. Today my son told me that he wants to live with me when he leaves Social Services Looked After Childrens Foster Care when he is 18 years old. I am delighted! Today I purchased my return train ticket to Birmingham for next Saturday's LGBT Pride. I aim to march with LGBTory.

Sunday 22nd May 2016

Dear Yvonne,
My beloved son James spoke to me via FaceTime in the early hours of this morning. It was hard for me to resume my sleep after speaking with him. This morning I was on Welcoming Duties at my local Brixton and Streatham Quaker Meeting for Worship. We couldn't get into the building today and held the meeting in the garden. It was Superb! Afterwards I spent time getting prepared for work near my workplace at the Thirsty Bear Pub and sipped Sparking Water with Lemon and Lime slices; then Tomato Juice and Wooster sauce. Work went very well today except for my last hour when I felt my brain starting to malfunction. I began to feel as if I was having a Nervous Breakdown. My brain felt as if it was short

circuiting. I left work one hour early and on arrival home took my anti-psychotic medication, had a bath and am now preparing to go to bed.

Monday 23rd May 2016

Dear Yvonne,
I didn't sleep well last night. Was awake for hours and woke up early this morning. I visited my GP and after asking me a series of questions, she signed me off work for one week - seven days starting today. My GP also asked me to have some blood tests done and told me to contact Primrose, my GP plus mental health worker. I left a voicemail for Primrose and her boss to return my call. I then went to work and handed in my sick note.

Tuesday 24th May 2016

Dear Yvonne,
My beloved son James spoke to me via FaceTime at 00:30hrs. Today I spent time at the Pump Chambers. Positive outcome. Closure. This evening I spoke to my son via FaceTime and he gave me a face to face visit.

Wednesday 25 May 2016

Dear Yvonne,
Today I slept for most of the day. This evening I was visited face to face by my beloved son James.

Thursday 26th May 2016

Dear Yvonne,
Today I participated in some Stonewall Role
Model Training and later listened to a Freemason
talk by Connie. I also spoke with my beloved son
via FaceTime.

Friday 27th May 2016

Dear Yvonne,
This morning I visited my solicitor. This evening I
was given a face to face visit by my beloved son
James.

Saturday 28th May 2016

Dear Yvonne,
Today I slept for most of the day. This evening my
beloved son visited me face to face.

Sunday 29th May 2016

Dear Yvonne,
Yesterday, I received a letter detailing my beloved
son James' last Social Service' review. This
morning I was still mulling over it's contents.
where it had described me as seemingly
'sabotaging the placement'. I spent ninety minutes
speaking on the phone to my dear friend Birgit
about it and in the end went for a cuppa in the
Ritzy Bar; to finally get on with my OU homework.
Just as I was settling into my homework a woman
approached me and asked if she could speak to

me. I rather irritatedly signal that she could. She told me that she was in a psychiatric ward with me and that I was writing a book and she has since seen me in a television advert about mental health. I told the woman that my book 'Altered Perceptions, 18 months one day at a time in the life of a mental health service user' was published in 2010. I also told her that I have not had a hospital admission since she last saw me. I invited her to sit and we chatted. She is currently an inpatient in Bethlem Royal Hospital, where she has been for years and is on the cusp of moving into shared housing in the community. We agreed to exchange numbers and meet in the Ritzy Bar in the future.

Monday 30th May 2016

Dear Yvonne,
This afternoon, I returned to work and after having a handover was taken for a Cuppa and a chat with my boss, Sydney. I think Sydney is a great boss; she soon settled me back into the work mode, after she made me feel welcomed back.

Tuesday 31st May 2016

Dear Yvonne,
Yesterday I spent a lovely day at work. I have really missed my clients and colleagues. Today I am delighted that Jeremy Swain, my Thames Reach Chief Executive tweeted my 2016 SANE/Huffington Post interview.

Wednesday 1st June 2016

Dear Yvonne,
This morning, I struggled to wake up, but was pleased it was a work day. Today was a Team Meeting day.

Thursday 2nd June 2016

Dear Yvonne,
Today seemed to be an especially busy day at work. I finished work at 22:30hrs and I am pleased my day off is tomorrow.

Friday 3rd June 2016

Dear Yvonne,
Today I slept on and off until the late afternoon. Then I took a stroll to the Ritzy Bar for a coffee and pizza. I stopped off on my route home to chat with Mrs Mills, my elderly neighbour and was formally introduced to her daughter Joan. Then just before I arrived home I met and spoke with Anthony Hoggard, my upstair neighbour.

Saturday 4th June 2016

Dear Yvonne,
Today I slept all morning and then visited a couple of friends in Dulwich. Together we went for lunch and a stroll in Peckham Rye with their dog. Today it was announced that the Boxer Mohammed Ali has died age 74. I was just coming to terms with

the fact that the musician/singer Prince has also died this year.

Sunday 5th June 2016

Dear Yvonne,
Today was a work day. In addition I received the offer of a Huffington Post Video Interview - relating to Schizophrenia to be in time for National Carers Week. I may be making the recording this Friday at the Huffington Post offices.

Monday 6th June 2016

Dear Yvonne,
Today was a work day. Today my beloved son James spoke with me via FaceTime. I am so pleased to hear and see him.

Tuesday 7th June 2016

Dear Yvonne,
Today was a work day. Today my beloved son spoke with me via FaceTime. I am so pleased. I have missed him so much.

Wednesday 8th June 2016

Dear Yvonne,
Today is my dear friend Birgit's birthday and my last work day for a for one week. Today I received another reminder via email from the Electoral Reform Society regarding being able to run online

non bias EU Referendum groups. This evening my beloved son James visited me face to face.

Thursday 9th June 2016

Dear Yvonne,
Today I spent most of the morning sleeping. This afternoon I had a cuppa and a snack in the Ritzy Bar; then did a small food shop in M&S before returning home. I received confirmation that I will be interviewed tomorrow. I spoke with my beloved son James via FaceTime this evening.

Friday 10th June 2016

Dear Yvonne,
Today I was interviewed on camera at the Huffington Post offices, for a mental health short vignette, wearing my new black with Stonewall Star, Stonewall Tee-shirt. This evening my beloved son James spoke with me via FaceTime and gave me a face to face visit.

Saturday 11th June 2016

Dear Yvonne,
This morning I felt too tired to attend my bicycle maintenance course. I spent the morning in bed. Then went to the Ritzy Bar, where I met a friend and went shopping.

Sunday 12th June 2016

Dear Yvonne,
This morning is Queen Elizabeth's official 90th
Birthday and I did a 5K walk in Crystal Palace
Stadium with the Pink Army for Cancer Research
UK. I completed my 5K walk in 59:20. Today I
spoke with my beloved son via FaceTime and this
evening he visited me face to face.

Monday 13th June 2016

Dear Yvonne,
Today is my annual day off. I am still so very sad,
deeply upset and heartbroken about the Orlando,
Florida USA shooting dead of 49 and injuring 53
people in a Gay Club. This evening I visited Old
Compton Street Soho and stopped off at a Gay
Twelve Step Meeting before joining with everyone
else present for the Vigil. Today my beloved son
James spoke with me via FaceTime and then
gave me a face to face visit.

Tuesday 14th June 2016

Dear Yvonne,
Today was my annual leave day off from work and
I officially deferred my OU-Open University
studies. This evening I attended a Conservative
Party, Parliamentary Boundary Briefing meeting in
the Betty Boothroyd room at Portcullis House and
I then went to CCHQ Conservative Campaign
Headquarters to do some phone canvassing for
Dan Watkins for the Tooting By-Election. I am
feeling less optimistic that if I am elected onto the

Conservatives Official Candidate list, I will be selected as a Parliamentary Candidate for Dulwich and West Norwood Conservatives. This is because it may sadly not exist after the forthcoming boundary changes. This evening I spoke with my beloved son James via FaceTime.

Wednesday 15th June 2016

Dear Yvonne,
Today I went back to work for the day; and also spoke with my son via FaceTime. This evening my beloved son James gave me a face to face visit.

Thursday 16th June 2016

Dear Yvonne,
Today was my annual leave day off. I spent the day relaxing in bed. Today I received a reply via email from Wes Streeting MP's intern that Wes would like to meet me for a Cuppa in Parliament. It is just a matter of when. Later via the radio I heard the awful news that the female Labour Politician Jo Cox MP, who is married with two young children aged three and five years, and was elected thirteen months ago in at the 2015 General Election, had been shot and stabbed in her constituency today and has died from her injuries.

Friday 17th June 2016

Dear Yvonne,
I feel so deeply saddened by the Orlando
occurrence, which was said to have been at the
hands of a practicing Muslim - in this, the midst of
Ramadan. The killer was someone who has
reportedly visited the premises on numerous
occasions and also engaged with Gay dating
apps. I am also sickened to the pit of my stomach
about the murder of Jo Cox MP. Today was my
day off. I met with my best female friend Birgit
Rapp and dined at a vegetarian and vegan cafe in
Catford. We then caught a bus to City Hall and
was taken on a tour of the building curtesy of GLR
LGBT Out in Unison. Today I found out that my
Lambeth Council has axed the Hate Crime
Policing Strategy, since 31st March 2016. This
evening I spoke with my son via FaceTime and
was also visited by him face to face.

Saturday 18th June 2016

Dear Yvonne,
Today was my day off. I spent the morning resting.
This afternoon I spoke with my beloved son
James via FaceTime. James then gave me a
official face to face contact. I am proud that I am
showcased amongst Sir Ian McKellen and others
on the official Stonewall website.

Sunday 19th June 2016

Dear Yvonne,
Today was a work day. I spoke to my beloved son James via FaceTime.

Monday 20th June 2016

Dear Yvonne,
Today was another work day. I also spoke to my beloved son James via FaceTime. Today I sent an email to Helen Hayes MP and various local Lambeth politicians to try to start the process of reinstating the Lambeth Hate Crime Initiative with the Police.

Tuesday 21st June 2016

Dear Yvonne,
Today is a work day. I spoke to my beloved son James via FaceTime and was visited by James before I went to work today. Jeremy Swain, my Thames Reach Chief Executive visited my hostel at work today. We got chatting about my standing for a Conservative Councillor - which was for the Coldharbour Ward in the 2010 and 2014 Lambeth Local Elections; plus my now aim to be the first black Openly Lesbian Conservative MP. Jeremy revealed to me that he is a long standing staunch Labour supporter.

Wednesday 22nd June 2016

Dear Yvonne,
I took today off as annual leave. My beloved son James talked to me via FaceTime twice this morning. Today is also the last day of campaigning for the EU Referendum Remain/Leave - Brexit, before tomorrow's election. I spent the morning sleeping. This afternoon, I met with Primrose, my GP Plus, Mental Health Professional for a pre-arranged Cuppa and a chat in the Ritzy Bar. Tomorrow, I aim to be present for a RSVP Metropolitan Archives film screening of 'Reel in the Closet', which will take place from 8pm to 9:30pm at the University of Westminster. This evening, I was given a face to face visit by my son.

Thursday 23rd June 2016

Dear Yvonne,
Last night there was a downpour of rain and flooding outside. The water leaked into my abode. Today is Polling Day from 7am to 10pm. This evening, I spoke to my son via FaceTime and then was visited face to face by him.

Friday 24th June 2016

Dear Yvonne,
Well, it is a historic day! The Great British Public has voted to Leave at 52% and Remain 48% out of an electorate of 72% Leave won by one million votes. Prime Minister David Cameron has resigned and a new Prime Minister is hoped to be

in post by the October 2016 Conservative Conference.

Saturday 25th June 2016

Dear Yvonne,
Today I attended a pre - London Pride brunch in Soho with my LGBTory members and then marched for the first time with LGBTory at the London Pride march. Two years ago I marched at London Pride with Stonewall for Stonewall UK's 25th Anniversary. This evening, I attended a talk by London Wide London Assembly Conservative Kemi Badenoch.

Sunday 26th June 2016

Dear Yvonne,
Today I attended Black Pride in Vauxhall Pleasure Gardens with LGBTory members and then went to work. Today I spoke with my beloved son James via FaceTime.

Monday 27th June 2016

Dear Yvonne,
This morning I spoke to my beloved son James via FaceTime. James then visited me face to face before I went to work today.

Tuesday 28th June 2016

Dear Yvonne,
Today is a work day. This morning I spoke to my beloved son James via FaceTime and then gave him a brief face to face visit before I went to work.

Wednesday 29th June 2016

Dear Yvonne,
Today was a Client Day shift at work. I started my day by visiting the Webber Street Day Centre - which is a London City Mission project; and ended the day by visiting the A&E Department at St Thomas' Hospital with one of my clients. I spoke to my beloved son James via FaceTime.

Thursday 30th June 2016

Dear Yvonne,
Today I had an annual leave day off from work. Slept all morning and visited my local Ritzy Bar for a Cuppa. I spoke with my beloved son James via FaceTime and then I was given a face to face visit from James.

Friday 1st July 2016

Dear Yvonne,
Today was my day off. I spent the morning sleeping and this afternoon, I visited the Ritzy Cinema to watch the film: Absolutely Fabulous: The Movie. I loved it! This evening I spoke with my beloved son James and I was given a face to face visit from James.

Saturday 2nd July 2016

Dear Yvonne,
Today was my day off. I spent the morning sleeping. This evening I spoke with my beloved son James via FaceTime and I was visited by James face to face.

Sunday 3rd July 2016

Dear Yvonne,
Last night I enjoyed a wonderful dream about my and C, the love of my life. I have been in love with her and loving her for almost twelve years to the exclusion of all others. Today I have an annual leave day off. I spoke with my beloved son James via FaceTime. This afternoon, I had a Cuppa at the Ritzy Bar. This evening James gave me a face to face visit.

Monday 4th July 2016

Dear Yvonne,
Today is a work day, plus Today is America's Independence Day and Nigel Farage has stepped down from his leadership role in UKIP.

Tuesday 5th July 2016

Dear Yvonne,
Today I have taken a annual day's leave from work. I spent most of the day resting and spoke with my beloved son James via FaceTime and then I was given a face to face visit by my son.

This evening, I attended a Dulwich & West Norwood Conservative Herne Hill and Coldharbour Wards branch meeting at the Fox on the Hill Pub.

Wednesday 6th July 2016

Dear Yvonne,
Today was a work day. I spoke with my beloved son James via FaceTime and then this evening I was given a face to face visit by my son.

Thursday 7th July 2016

Dear Yvonne,
Today I took an annual leave day from work. I spent the day resting and sleeping on and off in bed.

Friday 8th July 2016

Dear Yvonne,
Today was my day off. I visited the Ace of Clubs Day Centre and then had lunch in the Ritzy Bar. This evening I spoke to my beloved son James via FaceTime. James then gave me a face to face visit; and told me that today he received my seventeenth birthday present to him - his first driving lesson in a geared car. This will be the second time in James' life when he has driven. The first time was when he was aged ten and was taken on a contact visit with me to digger land; where he was given a driving lesson in a Land Rover 'automatic'. And lastly James flew a four seater aircraft when he was fourteen; this was a

birthday present from me. I am glad James enjoyed himself.

Saturday 9th July 2016

Dear Yvonne,
Today was my second day off. I spent the morning sleeping, then went for a cuppa at my local Ritzy Bar. This afternoon I spent just over one hour at the Ace of Clubs Day Centre's 21st Birthday Party. I ate and listened to live music. It was a great celebration. In addition I connected with another local Quaker Friend, who has skin cancer and conducted some Quaker Overseer pastoral care over a cup of coffee at Caffe Nero in Brixton. This evening there was a roadblocks for hours as 'BlackLivesMatters' demonstrators took their protest to the streets of Brixton. I spoke to my beloved son James via FaceTime and then James gave me a late brief face to face visit.

Sunday 10th July 2016

Dear Yvonne,
Before work today, I attended a Meeting for Worship at my local Brixton and Streatham Quaker Friends House and I was also on Welcoming duties. Today it was agreed by myself and other Overseers that I am to buy a pot plant for our Friend with skin Cancer. Today I also found out that JFLAG - the Jamaican Forum for Lesbian, Gay and All Sexuals are fundraising for Jamaica's forthcoming second LGBT PRIDE. Jamaica is the birthplace of my parents. PRIDEJA2016.

Monday 11th July 2016

Dear Yvonne,
Today Mrs Teresa May MP and Home Secretary
became the leader of my Conservative Party and
will now follow in Mrs Thatcher's steps and
become the UK's second female Prime minister.
Whilst at work, a journalist texted, tweeted and left
a voicemail for me regarding the possibilities of
me appearing with other mainly Conservative
Party members tomorrow morning on the BBC
Victoria Devonshire show. In the meantime, my
beloved son James FaceTimed, emailed and
messaged me and eventually has arranged to
meet with me for a Pizza this forthcoming
Wednesday evening.

Tuesday 12th July 2016

Dear Yvonne,
Last night I arrived home thirty minutes before
midnight. I plan to take it easy this morning, as I
don't think I will be home from work tonight any
earlier.

Wednesday 13th July 2016

Dear Yvonne,
I spoke to my beloved son via FaceTime just after
midnight. James was reminding me that he is
coming to give me a face to face visit after I finish
work today and we will be dining on Pizza. Today I
also had a very special supervision at work, which
included work/life balance. This afternoon David

Cameron officially stopped being the prime minister and Theresa May started.

Thursday 14th July 2016

Dear Yvonne,
Prior to going to work this morning I listened to one of my favourite talk radio host - namely LBC radio's Steve Allen. I experienced fits of laughter and was inspired to make another one of my own live online talk 'Heathen Massive' digital radio broadcasts. Incidentally as well as speaking with my beloved son James via FaceTime and given a face to face visit from him; Today was the first full day of Prime Minister Theresa May, in office.

Friday 15th July 2016

Dear Yvonne,
Today was my day off. This morning I collected 'Stella' my Stelazine sugar free anti-psychotic mental health medication from the chemist. I then spent this afternoon dining in a cafe and walking in the park, with my dear friend Laura. This evening I spoke with my beloved son via FaceTime and then he gave me a face to face visit.

Saturday 16th July 2016

Dear Yvonne,
Today was supposed to be an official contact day, which was pre-booked in 2015 for my son to spend quality time with me. However he did not arrive and I spent the whole evening miserable.

Sunday 17th July 2016

Dear Yvonne,
Today was a work day. I'm tired because I didn't sleep very well.

Monday 18th July 2016

Dear Yvonne,
Last night I slept better and it was business as usual for me at work today, except the day was one of intense heat.

Tuesday 19th July 2016

Dear Yvonne,
Today I had a Client/Specialism day at work. Got a fair amount done; although it was even hotter. This evening my beloved son James gave me a face to face visit.

Wednesday 20th July 2016

Dear Yvonne,
Today I attended my Team Away Day at the Ortus Centre at the Maudsley Psychiatric Hospital. I met WiL again. WiL was my old weekly Group Psychotherapy facilitator. During the day I bumped into David Taylor, Head of Pharmacy and he gave me a hug. David and I were both Schizophrenia Commission Commissioners. This evening, I met with my dear old friend Birgit and she took me for dinner and a chat. We dined Indian.

Thursday 21st July 2016

Dear Yvonne,
Today I officially started dating a Woman. I am in
an exclusive long term, long distance relationship
with her. Today I was a work day. This evening my
beloved son James gave me a face to face visit.

Friday 22nd July 2016

Dear Yvonne,
Today I worked an extra day. It is unusual for me
to work on a Friday, but I was just trying to help
out. My beloved son James spoke with me today
via FaceTime and was surprised that I was at
work. This evening I was shattered.

Saturday 23rd July 2016

Dear Yvonne,
Today was my day off. I slept for most of the
morning. Then I had brunch at The Ritzy Bar. This
afternoon I visited my dear friend Laura and her
partner Neville in Dulwich. I had a great time. This
evening I spent the time relaxing.

Sunday 24th July 2016

Dear Yvonne,
Today was my extra day off. It is in lieu for working
Friday. I spent most of the day in bed,
communicating with my partner. This evening my
beloved son spoke with me via FaceTime and
then gave me a face to face visit.

Monday 25th July 2016

Dear Yvonne,
Today was a work day. In particular a
Client/Specialism Day. It was another extremely
fulfilling and busy day. I spent most of this evening
communicating with my partner and finally fell
asleep around midnight.

Tuesday 26th July 2016

Dear Yvonne,
Today I took an annual days leave off from work. I
spent most of the day resting in bed. In the
evening, I went for a coffee at my local Ritzy Bar. I
then did a small food shop at M&S in Brixton.
Later this evening my beloved son James spoke
with me via FaceTime and then gave me a face to
face visit. I am in love with my partner and spent
some time today communicating this fact. She
also loves me in return and is a very different type
of woman, when compared to C. Besides, my love
of C was unrequited.

Wednesday 27th July 2016

Dear Yvonne,
Today was a work day. I started my shift with a
Supervision meeting with my manager. And since
it is Wednesday, I also participated in a Team
Meeting. By the time I arrived home this evening, I
felt shattered, brain dead and over stimulated. I
took a long hot silent candlelit bubble bath and
went straight to bed.

Thursday 28th July 2016

Dear Yvonne,
Today before work, I took three hours toil - time off in lieu and visited the West London NAZ offices to record my 1000Women website interview. Today my son's new Social Services Social Worker phoned me. We have agreed to meet in his International House office at 10am on Monday 1st August 2016. After work this evening, my beloved son James spoke to me via FaceTime and then gave me a face to face visit.

Friday 29th July 2016

Dear Yvonne,
Today was my day off. I visited the Ritzy Cinema and watched the feel good children's animation cartoon feature film: The Secret Life of Pets. I laughed a lot and really enjoyed it. At 16:00hrs I had a telephone conversation with a Amazon Radio Podcast Producer, regarding my suitability to be recorded for the topic of Schizophrenia. This podcast would be made available to the 244 million Amazon Audible Subscribers. It was left that I may be recorded next Friday. This evening my beloved son James gave me a Face To Face visit. In addition, today I also miscommunicated with my partner; and there have been unfortunate consequences.

Saturday 30th July 2016

Dear Yvonne,
Last night I didn't sleep well due to the situation between my partner and myself. It is my day off. I had brunch at my local Ritzy Bar. This afternoon I was also assisted by way of a lift in a car by a local neighbour to visit B&Q in Croydon; on a mission as a Quaker Overseer, to buy an Olive Tree for a fellow quaker friend from my meeting house, who is poorly with Cancer. This evening I was visited by my beloved son for an official Unsupervised Contact.

Sunday 31st July 2016

Dear Yvonne,
I had another poor night's sleep. Today is a work day. I am desperately saddened by what has manifested within my relationship with my partner; and I am perfectly clear that I am partly responsible.

Monday 1st August 2016

Dear Yvonne,
This morning before going to work, I had a 10am meeting at International House with my son's new Social Services Social Worker. I tried to be compus mentus and coherent but I didn't arrive home from work until approximately midnight and by the time I got to sleep… Anyway I think the meeting went well. Following this meeting I briefly visited my Solicitor's office and then went for lunch at The Ritzy Bar. My adorable partner rang and

spoke with me today. It was so unexpected and created such a thrill for me. Today I started my work day in Croydon, clothes shopping with a client.

Tuesday 2nd August 2016

Dear Yvonne,
Today was a work day. I felt tired, so spent the morning sleeping in bed and communicating with my partner; before work.

Wednesday 3rd August 2016

Dear Yvonne,
This morning before work, my partner rang and spoke with me. It was wonderful to hear her voice. I had a Supervision Meeting with my manager today at work. Also at the hostel, we had a barbacue. Wednesday are always busy because not only do we have our usual Handover Meetings, but we also have our Team Meeting. I spent most of the day in low spirits because was hoping to hear from my beloved son James, but he has not contacted me so far this week.

Thursday 4th August 2016

Dear Yvonne,
Today was a work day and I felt so tired. Today the Amazon Radio Producer rang me and has arranged to record me next Friday. I didn't hear from my beloved son James today. I spent the

evening after work communicating with my partner.

Friday 5th August 2016

Dear Yvonne,
Today was my day off. I spent the morning sleeping. Lunch time I visited The Ritzy Bar and in the afternoon I dined in Kaspar's Ice Cream Parlour with my dear old friend Birgit Rapp. This evening my beloved son James spoke to me via FaceTime and then gave me a face to face visit. I am delighted.

Saturday 6th August 2016

Dear Yvonne,
Today was my day off. I spent the morning and afternoon sleeping. I managed to do some laundry and a touch of Ironing, this evening.

Sunday 7th August 2016

Dear Yvonne,
Today was a work day. This morning I didn't attend a Quaker Meeting for Worship. I communicated with my partner. Had a great day.

Monday 8th August 2016

Dear Yvonne,
Today I spent much time communicating with my partner. I'm am loving being in a relationship with her. It is very different to C, because my partner [J] loves me back and lets me know in no

uncertain terms. Where as with C, it was definitely Unrequited Love. Today was a busy day at work.

Tuesday 9th August 2016

Dear Yvonne,
I am discovering my Erotomania - Love addiction, traits are very pronounced within my relationship with J. I accept that I am a Love Addict and I am sure that I am definitely not a sex addict. Pressure is not letting up on the work front.

Wednesday 10th August 2016

Dear Yvonne,
Today I heard from my beloved son James via FaceTime and he gave me a face to face visit this evening. I am delighted; also J mentioned to me that she is a little poorly today and quite naturally I want to cocoon J in a bubble of love and affection.

Thursday 11th August 2016

Dear Yvonne,
Today was an extremely busy day at work. I am glad that it's my day off tomorrow. My partner J, also works very hard and I am so proud of her. I respect J and love her a great deal. In my opinion J is the most important, beautiful and special woman to me who is alive. Today J received her detective status added to her badge. This evening my beloved son James spoke with me via FaceTime and then gave me a face to face visit.

Friday 12th August 2016

Dear Yvonne,
Today is my day off. This morning, I was
interviewed in my local Park by Ben, the Amazon
Radio Producer. The topic was Schizophrenia.
The edited recording will be available on Podcast
around September/October 2016. This evening I
dined in the Ritzy Bar and then watch a Jason
Bourne Film in the cinema. This evening my
beloved son James spoke with me via FaceTime
and then gave me a face to face visit. This
evening once James had left, I spent some quality
time communicating with my partner.

Saturday 13th August 2016

Dear Yvonne,
Today is my day off and it is also an Official
Contact Day for my beloved son James to visit
me. I was pleased to see him arrive and we spent
several hours of quality time, as usual. Today we
listened to Jazz music on Jazz FM radio and
intermittently chatted, ate and have a good time. It
is my opinion that James is the most important,
handsome, intelligent and hardworking man to me
that is alive. I am so proud of James.

Sunday 14th August 2016

Dear Yvonne,
This morning I attended my local Quaker Meeting
for Worship, before going to work. I also
communicated with my partner.

Monday 15th August 2016

Dear Yvonne,
This morning I was so tired. Work was also especially busy. I was pleased to be able to communicate with my loving, understanding partner; and my friends.

Tuesday 16th August 2016

Dear Yvonne,
This morning I visited my solicitor before work. I also spoke to my partner when she called.

Wednesday 17th August 2016

Dear Yvonne,
This morning my GP+ Mental Health, Third Sector Professional rang and spoke with me this morning. She offered me the opportunity to write a short contribution for the Annual Report; but it needs to be submitted before this Friday. Today I had supervision with my manager. It is going to be reduced to fortnightly. This afternoon my partner called and spoke with me. Wonderful. This evening a issue presented itself regarding my beloved son James. I left work early but the crisis was averted. My beloved son James gave me a face to face visit, following a couple of emails and a few messages. I also was in communication with my partner.

Thursday 18th August 2016

Dear Yvonne,
Today I woke with a headache, which lasted until
16:00hrs. Today I submitted my short story for the
GP+ Annual Report. My beloved son James,
spoke with me via FaceTime. I worked a long day,
from 12:00hrs until 22:30hrs. I spent time
communicating with my partner into the early
hours.

Friday 19th August 2016

Dear Yvonne,
This morning at 09:00, I was woken by my
partner's phone call. Both of us spent two and a
half hours, of quality time talking and listening to
each other. It was exquisitely blissful. Today I
found out that my GP+ Annual Report submission
was appreciated and will be included. I then
stopped off at my local Ritzy Bar for a flat white
coffee before I briefly went into work for
approximately one hour. My beloved son James
spoke to me via FaceTime and then gave me a
face to face visit. I did a bit of laundry this evening.

Saturday 20th August 2016

Dear Yvonne,
Today was my day off. I visited a travel agency in
Victoria and am looking into spending seven
nights in Barbados during November. I plan to
spend one night in Jamaica to visit my partner and
offer some support to JFLAG. I spent most of
today communicating with my partner. I also

visited my local Ritzy Bar for a Flat White Coffee. In addition I dined this evening in a Japanese restaurant. Also my beloved son James spoke with me via FaceTime and then gave me a face to face visit. This evening my partner communicated to me that she wanted to convey the greeting salutation of 'Hi' to my son. I told him and his reply to her was 'Hello', They both last met each other fourteen years ago. Today James told me that his placement of ten years has broken down, and he has been told by his new social worker three days ago that he is to be moved to a hostel.

Sunday 21st August 2016

Dear Yvonne,
Today while I was seated in the Ritzy sipping coffee and preparing for work, my partner [J] communicated that today is our one month anniversary. She also rang and spoke with me at three separate times throughout today. I have also changed my mind, and I'm now planning to spend seven day in Barbados with my partner; in November. Today while at work, I submitted my annual leave request, for November, to my manager.

Monday 22nd August 2016

Dear Yvonne,
Today I spoke with and communicated with my partner. There was also the very good news that my beloved son James spoke with me via FaceTime and has arranged to meet me at the

end of my evening shift on Wednesday. Today I sent self images of me wearing mostly Stonewall t-shirts to JFLAG. They were well received. I invited JFLAG to use my name and images to their advantage.

Tuesday 23rd August 2016

Dear Yvonne,
Today I sadly did not communicate very much with my partner, because her phone had technical issues. Today I registered my intention to attend a LGBTory Women's drinks, with Margot James in Soho on Wednesday 21st September 2016.

Wednesday 24th August 2016

Dear Yvonne,
I had early morning conversations and communications with my partner before setting off to work today. She was promoted in her employment yesterday and is starting her new job role today. I am so proud of her; as well as adoring her so much.   On arrival to work, I found that I had received a email from my Thames Reach Chief Executive/CEO; inviting me to support him at a Mental Health Festival event at the Houses of Parliament, on Tuesday 13th September 2016. Of course, I accepted. In addition, today I received a personal email from my Conservative Party informing me that I have now advanced to the next stage of the rigorous robust recruitment price of my application to be an

Official Conservative Party Candidate. I will need to succeed if I am to stand any chance of achieving being the first Black Openly Lesbian Conservative Member of Parliament to take my seat after the 2020 General Election. Today my beloved son James, sent me two emails, FaceTimed me twice, messaged me twice and then gave me a face to face visit.

Thursday 25th August 2016

Dear Yvonne,
Today at work, was a very sad day indeed. A client was found dead in his room by one of my colleagues. Last year, I found one of my clients dead in one of the bathrooms. It was deeply unsettling and disturbing, for staff and residents alike. So much professional human kindness is invested in each client, with the aim of eradicating the scourge of low expectation and aspiration for each one. Death is not an option, to be explored or sampled.Today was surreal with extreme busyness at the same time as it appeared to be going in slow motion. I peaked at about 19:30hrs and left work thirty minutes early. This evening I spoke with my beloved son James via FaceTime and then was given a face to face visit by him. I was also in intermittent communication with my partner throughout today.

Friday 26th August 2016

Dear Yvonne,
Last night I was up until 04:00hrs chatting and communicating with my partner. Today is my day off. I received a letter from my House of Commons MP, Helen Hayes; regarding an enquiry which I asked her to look in to, regarding reinstating the Crime Strategy initiative in Lambeth Council. This afternoon I spoke with my beloved son James via FaceTime and this evening, he gave me a face to face visit.

Saturday 27th August 2016

Dear Yvonne,
Today was supposed to be an official Contact with my beloved son James. However he is away with his foster parents.

Sunday 28th August 2016

Dear Yvonne,
Today I attended a quaker meeting for worship before going to work.

Monday 29th August 2016

Dear Yvonne,
Today is a bank holiday, and I am working. Missing my son but communicating with my partner.

Tuesday 30th August 2016

Dear Yvonne,
Today I was very tired at work.

Wednesday 31st August 2016

Dear Yvonne,
Today I had supervision with my manager. Then after the Handover Meeting the team met away from the hostel for a special Reflective Meeting, due to the recent death. This meeting was facilitated by Will Pennycook, she is my former psychologist of twelve years ago who facilitated my weekly group meetings. I told Will about my recently established reciprocated relationship. Will seemed pleased.

Thursday 1st September 2016

Dear Yvonne,
Today my beloved son James sent me an email. I was pleased to hear from him. I'm thinking about taking a one year unpaid sabbatical leave from work. Today my son's social work rang to tell me that my son is about to start a college course and that his placement has broken down and my son will be moving from his foster parent's home at some point. Hopefully not to Kent but somewhere near his college.

Friday 2nd September 2016

Dear Yvonne,
Today I have been communicating and speaking with my partner. I have also been preparing for my forthcoming seven night November 2016 break in Barbados. This evening my beloved son James spoke to me via FaceTime and then gave me a face to face visit. I am over joyed. Also there was a some dialogue between my partner and son via me this evening.

Saturday 3rd September 2016

Dear Yvonne,
Today was my day off. I spent my time doing laundry and reading in the Ritzy Bar.

Sunday 4th September 2016

Dear Yvonne,
Today I attended a Quaker Meeting for Worship before going to work. I spoke with my partner and had a great day.

Monday 5th September 2016

Dear Yvonne,
Today was a very busy work day. I was pleased to return to my bed at the end of it.

Tuesday 6th September 2016

Dear Yvonne,
This morning before work, I went to my favourite 'watering hole' i.e The Ritzy Bar. There I had my usual flat white coffee and water and sat communicating with my partner before going to work.

Wednesday 7th September 2016

Dear Yvonne,
This evening, my son spoke with me via FaceTime and then gave me a face to face visit.

Thursday 8th September 2016

Dear Yvonne,
Today after work, I attended a Dulwich and West Norwood Conservatives Executive Meeting, in Dulwich.

Friday 9th September 2016

Dear Yvonne,
Today was my day off. I spent most of the day in communications with my partner. In addition, I met with Primrose my GP Plus Mental Health worker. My beloved son James also spoke with me via FaceTime and then gave me a face to face visit.

Saturday 10th September 2016

Dear Yvonne,
Today I had an official face to face contact with my beloved son James. We spent several hours of quality time, chatting, eating and cuddling.

Sunday 11th September 2016

Dear Yvonne,
Today I attended a Meeting for Worship before going to work. I also spoke with my partner.

Monday 12th September 2016

Dear Yvonne,
Today was a work day and my partner also had a tooth extraction which was very painful for her. I felt powerless to support her effectively; and spent a very sleepless night.

Tuesday 13th September 2016

Dear Yvonne,
Today it is exactly one calendar month from my next birthday. This afternoon I visited the House of Lords, to hear Jeremy Swain, my Chief Executive speak at a Mental Health Festival event 'Mental Health and Homelessness. Also present was Paul Farmer, the CEO of MIND, and Lord John Bird, the founder of The Big Issue.

Wednesday 14th September 2016

Dear Yvonne,
Today I was back at work in my hostel. This evening I accompanied two clients to watch a Young Vic theatre performance of: The Emperor.

Thursday 15th September 2016

Dear Yvonne,
This evening after work I was visited by my beloved son James.

Friday 16th September 2016

Dear Yvonne,
Today was my day off. I spent the morning sipping coffee and water at the Ritzy Bar and communicating with my partner. In the afternoon I had lunch at a local Buddhist Centre in Kennington with my dear old friend Birgit. This evening my beloved son James visited me and my partner rang while he was with me and dedicated the Gwen Guthrie song, 'I'll give my best to you' to me, and serenaded me with it, over the phone. Oooh She is so romantic.

Saturday 17th September 2016

Dear Yvonne,
Today my partner and I were in almost constant contact, because she had to return to the dentist to have a splinter of tooth removed from her gum.

Today my beloved son James spent the whole day with me. It was wonderful.

Sunday 18th September 2016

Dear Yvonne,
Today I spent the morning in bed. This afternoon I went to work.

Monday 19th September 2016

Dear Yvonne,
Today my partner and I remained in communication because she went for a full health check.

Tuesday 20th September 2016

Dear Yvonne,
Today I was on a late shift at work. I spent some of the morning communicating with my beloved son James and my partner.

Wednesday 21st September 2016

Dear Yvonne,
Today is the anniversary of the second month in a relationship with my precious partner. We remained in contact. This evening, I attended a LGBTory Women's event where I was delighted to meet Margot James MP and hear her speak.

Thursday 22nd September 2016

Dear Yvonne,
Today I arrived at work at 08:30hrs. It was a very busy day and I left work at 18:00hrs. This evening I spent some quality time with my beloved son James, as he gave me a face to face visit. Also at different times throughout the day I communicated with my partner.

Friday 23rd September 2016

Dear Yvonne,
I spent the whole of last night in the company of my partner. I didn't rise from my bed until after midday. This afternoon I spent about one hour visiting my friend Laura, her partner Neville and her dog Bonnie. Then I briefly visited my dear old friend Birgit. This evening I spent with my beloved son James. Throughout today I communicated with my partner.

Saturday 24th September 2016

Dear Yvonne,
I spent most of today with my beloved son James. I also spent it communicating with my partner.

Sunday 25th September 2016

Dear Yvonne,
This morning before I went to work, I was on Welcoming duties, for Meeting for Worship at my local Quaker Friends Meeting House. By the time I

had finished my work duty shift in the evening, I was shattered.

Monday 26th September 2016

Dear Yvonne,

Today I was on a late duty shift at work. It was busy, as usual and seemed as if there was hardly enough hours in the day to complete the outstanding tasks.

Tuesday 27th September 2016

Dear Yvonne,
Last night I spent the evening in communication with my partner. It feels wonderful to be loved by her. She is so romantic.

Wednesday 28th September 2016

Dear Yvonne,
Today I collected my repeat prescription from the local chemist; and paid a few bills. I then went to work and enjoyed my Team Meeting.

Thursday 29th September 2016

Dear Yvonne,
This evening, after I finished my shift. My beloved son James visited me. We spent some quality time together. In the evening my son and my partner communicated with each other.

Friday 30th September 2016

Dear Yvonne,
This afternoon, I was visited by a first cousin's
adult son. This evening my beloved son James
visited me.

Saturday 1st October 2016

Dear Yvonne,
Today signifies the start of the 'Black History
Month' celebration. October also contains 'World
Mental Health Day' on the the tenth. Today I was
again visited by my cousin's son and this time my
beloved son James was also present. The cousins
had not seen each other for almost six years.

Sunday 2nd October 2016

Dear Yvonne,
This morning I did an early shift, for the first time in
a very long time. So I missed my Quaker Meeting
for Worship. This evening after work, I visited an
NA - Narcotics Anonymous Twelve Step Meeting
in my local Brixton Coldharbour Ward.

Monday 3rd October 2016
Dear Yvonne,

Today I was on a late shift at work. This evening I
communicated with my partner, as usual.

Tuesday 4th October 2016

Dear Yvonne,
Today while I was at work, I received a call from my son's social worker. He told me that tomorrow my son is going to view his new home and that he will be leaving his current foster parents this Friday. He has invited me to help James move and will phone me again tomorrow afternoon.

Wednesday 5th October 2016

Dear Yvonne,
Tonight after work, I communicated with my partner. Following which my son contacted me via FaceTime and we spoke for approximately an hour.

Thursday 6th October 2016

Dear Yvonne,
Today James' social worker left me a message to say that my son will be moving tomorrow and I will need to arrive at his foster parents at 11am tomorrow to help him move. This evening, my beloved son James visited me. James seemed to be in good spirits about his forthcoming move.

Friday 7th October 2016

Dear Yvonne,
At 11am this morning, I arrived at James' foster placement and with the assistance of his social worker and foster father, helped my son to move

to shared supportive housing in Thornton Health. On the 29th September 2016, James celebrated his tenth anniversary of living with his current foster carers in their home. Today after booking James into his new home, James followed me back to my home and spent the rest of the day with me.

Saturday 8th October 2016

Dear Yvonne,
This morning I was visited by T one of my first cousin's sons. It was lovely to see T. Then this afternoon, my beloved son James visited and spent the whole day. We went shopping together in Iceland and in the evening with his twenty pounds allowance for his weekly food shop at his new placement.

Sunday 9th October 2016

Dear Yvonne,
Today was a work day. It was an extremely challenging day. When I arrived home I spent time speaking with my partner.

Monday 10th October 2016

Dear Yvonne,
Today is World Mental Health Day. I spent the day at work. I also received a text message from Birgit, my dear old friend wishing me a happy WMHD 2016.

Tuesday 11th October 2016

Dear Yvonne,
Today I took an annual leave day off from work to attend my local branch Coldharbour/Herne Hill Wards Dulwich and West Norwood Conservative Association Meeting. However it was cancelled this morning. This afternoon, I was treated to lunch at the BlueBrick Cafe in Dulwich by my dearest old friend Birgit for my pre birthday celebration. It was lovely.

Wednesday 12th October 2016

Dear Yvonne,
Today was a work day and I was on a mid-shift. It was an extremely busy day and I left work half an hour later than I was due to.

Thursday 13th October 2016

Dear Yvonne,
Today is my birthday. In the early hours of this morning, my partner was the first person to wish me a happy birthday and then later I had birthday greetings from Quaker friends, political party friends, neighbour, work colleagues, friends, family. I worked today and my work colleagues and clients gave me a card, a chocolate cake and sang me happy birthday. This evening, T visited and gave me a card and chocolates and then my beloved son James visited and spent time with me and left after 22:30hrs.

Friday 14th October 2016

Dear Yvonne,
This morning I was up earlier than I really wanted
to be because I had housing repairs to be carried
out. I then had an appointment with the dentist
and hygienist. Then I went to work. Today very
sadly one of my hostel clients died. This is the
second client to have died since the first of August
2016. Clients and staff are finding this situation
very hard to cope with emotionally.

Saturday 15th October 2016

Dear Yvonne,
Today my beloved son James visited. He arrived
soaked with rain water and needed to borrow one
of my oversized jeans and a hoodie. James had
pushed a wheelchair bound elderly woman up the
hill after her electric wheelchair failed to operate in
the rain. James spent the night at my place and I
informed his placement. This is the first time
James and I - Mother and Son, had slept under
the same roof for just over eleven years. James
was taken into local authority care due to my
mental health difficulties.

Sunday 16th October 2016

Dear Yvonne,
Today is my annual leave day off work. I spent the
morning with my son. Both he and I spent the
night talking to each other, and I also spoke with
my partner. This morning my son and I went

shopping to spend his thirty pounds shopping for food in Iceland and M&S and then I left him on a bus making his way back to his placement with his shopping; while I went to an Area Elders and Overseers Meeting at my local Streatham and Brixton Friends Meeting House. This afternoon I was again visited by my son, as he had left his key at my place. James told me that he was delighted with his shopping and that he was glad to have a full fridge.

Monday 17th October 2016

Dear Yvonne,
Today I was very busy at work, as usual. Definitely grieving at work. I am however receiving lots of support from my partner and friends.

Tuesday 18th October 2016

Dear Yvonne,
Today I took an annual leave day from work. Today my beloved son James came to visit me. I was informed that there is Crack and Cannabis smoking taking place at his placement. I left James at my place while I attended this evening's Dulwich and West Norwood Conservative Association Social Evening, in Dulwich. Great Turn out.

Wednesday 19th October 2016

Dear Yvonne,
Today I went back to work, and bereaved team, who one and all in today's team meeting seemed somber and appeared drained. After work this evening I attended a LGBT+ Conservatives Fish and Chips Fundraiser with the Rt. Hon. Justine Greening MP in Whitehall. There was a great turn out and I was most impressed with the speech that Justine made.

Thursday 20th October 2016

Dear Yvonne,
Today I was a bit tired at work, but I felt great to be able to support my clients and colleagues. This evening my beloved son James visited and so did T, my first cousin's son.

Friday 21st October 2016

Dear Yvonne,
Today was my day off. I feel very tired. trying to rest. I am spending lots of time communicating with my partner, son and friends.

Saturday 22nd October 2016

Dear Yvonne,
This morning I met with a photographer at the Tate Modern to take photos to accompany my 1000Women online interview. This afternoon I treated myself to a Indian Head Massage with

Margherita at the Brixton Therapy Centre. It was amazing. This evening my beloved son James came to visit. He is finding his drug crazed placement preposterous. James slept over. While with me, James spoke to one of his Rudolf Steiner school friends, on his phone and seemed a bit better.

Sunday 23rd October 2016

Dear Yvonne,
Before I went to work today, I took my beloved son James to do his weekly shopping. We met with S one of my first cousins in M&S and had a brief catch up chat. Then I ensured that James was safely on the bus to his placement. James left a few of his garments behind and I found myself washing clothes that belongs to my son, for the first time in over eleven years.

Monday 24th October 2016

Dear Yvonne,
Today we were extra busy and as we are also under staffed at work, it is very demanding. We have great managers and a fantastic team. I feel privileged to be a Support Worker for Thames Reach.

Tuesday 25th October 2015

Dear Yvonne,
This morning I got up at 5am to get ready for a morning at City Hall for the Health Commission for LGBT Mental Health, after having arrived home

from work at almost midnight and not falling asleep until 02:00. It was a great turn out at the event. I then went for a facial, pedicure and manicure at Blackheath Day Spa. This is a treat for myself. Today I also bought a few bits and pieces i.e. clothes for my forthcoming six night holiday in Barbados with my partner. This evening T, my first cousins' son visited me.

Wednesday 26th October 2016

Dear Yvonne,
Today was a work day and some of it was spent reflecting on the recent death of the client and past clients. This evening I spent speaking with my beloved son James and my partner.

Thursday 27th October 2016

Dear Yvonne,
Today is my annual day's leave. I have taken today off in preparation of a trip to Cambridge tomorrow.

Friday 28th October 2016

Dear Yvonne,
Today I spent in Cambridge. On my return to London, this evening my beloved son spoke to me via FaceTime to say that there has been a stabbing at his placement and someone had smashed the front window there and the police are on the premises and someone had told my son to hold on to a couple of machetes. I reported this

and the police confiscated them. My son my have to attend a court case regarding this matter. Tonight it makes exactly three weeks since my son has moved into this placement. The police also advised my son that he should stay somewhere else for a few days. By the time my son came to stay with me via a taxi it was about 2am; and my son had not eaten all day. Quite naturally I sent a disapproving email to my son's social worker and support worker.

Saturday 29th October 2016

Dear Yvonne,
My son stayed awake the whole night and finally went to sleep in my bed at 10am. My son wrote an email to his old foster parents. It was chilling. I have rung my workplace and told them that I will not be at work tomorrow or Monday, as I need to take special leave. My son slept all day until approximately 6pm and a woke briefly to speak with my partner on the phone. Neither my partner or I slept a wink last night. I am stressed and bemused; and my beloved son is traumatised. I am dedicated to nurturing my beloved son. I love him more than anything or one else in this world.

Sunday 30th October 2016

Dear Yvonne,
Today the clocks went back one hour at two o'clock this morning. I woke at 6am and had a bath and my son, who had been awake all night, went to sleep in my bed. This evening I ran my

son a lovely candlelit hot bubble bath and dined
on a gourmet beef burger, fries and a milkshake.

Monday 31st October 2016

Dear Yvonne,
Today I rang and spoke with my son's support
worker's manager; who told me that he will call me
back with more details. In addition I visited the
Social Services Department to try to speak with
my son's social worker; but he was not present, a
message was left for him to return my call. I also
spoke to my manager, and she said that she
would email my son's social worker and support
worker on my behalf. I then rang my dear friend
Brigit and explained what is happening. Brigit was
alarmed and said that she would be happy to keep
my son's company for eight or nine hours while I
go to work.

Tuesday 1st November 2016

Dear Yvonne,
Last night, my son and I slept from 16:00hrs to
01:00hrs. We spoke with each other for a while
and then I went back to bed until 07:30hrs. Today
I again visited the Social Services' department at
International House. My son's social worker is
away this week and I spoke with a duty worker;
who said that my son can stay with me until they
find another placement for him. I was delighted. I
then went for a flat white coffee at my favourite
watering hole i.e. The Ritzy Bar and reflected.

Then I went home and told my son, who was also very happy. I then went to the Travel Agents and booked an extra place on my flight and Sugar Bay Resort hotel for my son to be with me and my partner from next Thursday. I then rang my manager and confirmed that I will be going back to work tomorrow morning. In addition, I took control of my son's BSM - British School of Motoring driving lessons and changed his address to my own and booked a lesson for him, for the Monday after we return from our six nights holiday in Barbados. This evening, my son had a shave and then we went for a walk locally. My son's placement manager rang this evening and mentioned that my son and I can view a new placement tomorrow. I told him that I would do so after work.

Wednesday 2nd November 2016

Dear Yvonne,
This morning, I went to work and my manager gave me another carers special leave day off from work. She told me to come back tomorrow at noon for supervision. I left work and went straight to social services' International House. I met with two duty officers and and amongst other thing they told me that a higher manager would have to grant my son's passport release for a trip with me to Barbados. I went home and told my son. Just as my son and I was getting ready to leave my abode to view his potential new accommodation; a manager rang and told me that my request had been denied by her. My son tried to appeal to this manager but she refused to allow him to have his

passport to allow him to travel to Barbados. My son, my partner and myself were all extremely disappointed and angry. The manager told me that I should not have booked that ticket. my son is under a full care order, no one had said that he could reside with me and I had not been accessed. After this phone call, my son and I went to view this new placement which is based in Streatham, which is much closer than Thornton Heath. Both my son and I liked it. We walked home after viewing it. I agreed that I would move my son in this Sunday. I then called BSM and arranged for my son to start taking his driving lessons from his new abode as of this Monday. I then took a bus to Thornton Heath and packed and collected my son's possessions and took them back to my place to wash. Both my son and I was shattered and fell asleep at around 18:00hrs.

Thursday 3rd November 2016

Dear Yvonne,
This morning, I sent an email to Helen Hayes, my MP and my Lambeth Conservative Council Leader to see if they could help to allow my son to fly. I also visited International House again, to try to find out if the manager of the manager who rang yesterday would be able to change the decision. The head of service was also called but neither were answering their phone. I then went to work and spoke of my anguish with my Thames Reach manager. She told me to take two additional Carers special leave days off and return after my holiday, but phone her on the Friday before my

Sunday shift. On my way home, I sent an email to my Thames Reach Chief Executive to see if there is anything that he could do to help. I also contacted the Ombudsman, explained my situation and secured a reference number; in addition I made an official online complaint to Lambeth Council. I then went home to spend time with my son and commence washing his clothes. Lastly I left messages on the voicemail boxes of the social services' manager' manager who denied my son and the Head of Service. The only person, who I have heard from today regarding this issue is my Lambeth Conservative Council Leader; who was looking into launching an urgent inquiry. I also heard from my Conservative London Assembly politician, my friend Birgit and my partner.

Friday 4th November 2016

Dear Yvonne,
Today is my day off. I got showered, had my breakfast and arrived at International House for just after 09:30hrs. I obtained the email addresses of the Service Manager and the Head of Service and sent them both an email. Then I went for a cup of flat white at my favourite watering hole. By the time, I arrived home I found that I had received an email from my Thames Reach CEO, acknowledging my son's ordeal and asking how he can help. Before I had time to reflect on his question, I received an email from the Social Services Service Manager. For the first time it now seems as if it is possible that my son will be going to Barbados with me. My son, was heartened by

the news. I then went to the travel agents to obtain the non electronic flight ticket. While I was there, I received a telephone call from my son's social worker's line manager. She said that a meeting is taking place this Monday regarding my son's placement service provider and asked if it would be okay for my son to continue to reside with me beyond this Sunday, as my son may be placed with another service provider. I said that my son can stay with me as long as he needs to. I asked her if my son can now come to Barbados with me. She said that it may be possible, but she will call again. She also asked about my son's wellbeing. On my way home I shopped in M&S and came home and changed the pick up location for my son's Monday BSM driving lessons, while my son listened to music while reading from his iPad. I am shattered, and I am just about to run a lovely hot candlelit bubble bath.

Saturday 5th November 2016

Dear Yvonne,
Yesterday evening, I was cc'd into an email from Clapham Common, Lambeth Conservative Opposition Leader Councillor Tim Briggs, requesting a URGENT Members Inquiry for Permission for my son to go on holiday. This morning I took a train ride to Luton. In the afternoon, I watched the film: Nocturnal Animals, at the Ritzy Cinema and in the evening I did some of my son's laundry and relaxed indoors with him. James has now been residing with me for one whole week.

Sunday 6th November 2016

Dear Yvonne,
Today I was woken by my son waking up and going for a walk at 06:30hrs. On his return he made a couple of long phone calls and sounded happy. I finally got up at 09:30hrs and continued doing a bit of my suitcase packing for Barbados. I then went for scrambled eggs on toast with a flat white coffee breakfast at in The Ritzy Bar. I invited my son, but he declined because he had already eaten. This afternoon, I bumped into Vassall Ward, Lambeth Labour Councillor Jacqui Dyer in my favourite Brixton. We had a friendly chat. Throughout the day, I have been communicating with my partner.

Monday 7th November 2016

Dear Yvonne,
Today, my son woke at 06:00hrs and took a walk. I woke at 09:00hrs, ate breakfast and then went for a flat white coffee in The Ritzy Bar. I then went to collect my son's and my itinerary and tickets from the Travel Agents. This afternoon my son was called by his social worker; who also spoke with me and told me that James CAN go on holiday with me to Barbados. The social worker also said that it is possible that James can continue to reside with me, however we can talk about that tomorrow when I see the social worker at International House at 10am. I am delighted and have been emailing my thanks to everybody that has helped me and my son with this issue.

This evening, my son went out for another walk. He seems to be recovering and is a lot happier than I have seen him in some considerable time.

Tuesday 8th November 2016

Dear Yvonne,
This morning I went to International House. I received a confirmation letter for my son's social worker that I can take my son abroad. I also informed my son's social worker that my son would like to move in to the Streatham Inclusive Care Placement for a few months to prepare him to find his independence before leaving the care system. I then went to Streatham and collected my son's passport and his provisional driving licence.

Wednesday 9th November 2016

Dear Yvonne,
Today is the last day to get things done before my six nights in Barbados. This morning my son went off to an appointment with the Princes' Trust and I went to my usual watering hole for a flat white coffee. This afternoon, I booked tickets for my son and I to attend Vauxhall Conservatives Xmas drinks with the Rt Hon Jeremy Hunt MP and I also booked tickets for my son and I to attend the London LGBT+ Conservatives Xmas drinks. I attended an appointment with Primrose, my GP+ Mental Health Nurse and My partner rang me and told me that she is ready for our holiday. This evening my son went for a two hour driving lesson, while I finished packing my suitcase. My

son has requested a pizza tonight. Then I am going to support my son to pack his suitcase and then I'll have a hot bubble bath and prepare for an early start. My son and I need to be at Gatwick tomorrow for 10.00hrs.

Friday 18th November 2016

Dear Yvonne,
My son and I arrived back in the UK, from a six nights holiday in Barbados with my partner yesterday morning. We are still jet lagged. This morning, I rang my manager and told her that my son will continue to reside with me and I will be returning to work this Sunday.

Saturday 19th November 2016

Dear Yvonne,
Last night I slept, on and off for approximately eighteen hours. Today I got up and went shopping. This evening, my son went to visit a Rudolf Steiner school mate.

Sunday 20th November 2016

Dear Yvonne,
My beloved son, returned home with his Rudolf Steiner school friend at 04:00hrs. They were both soaked to the skin with rain water and looked so cute. Just as I remembered them both at ages three or four years old. Today is a work day and

before I go to work, I have an appointment with the dentist and the hygienist.

Monday 21st November 2016

Dear Yvonne,
Yesterday I received a filling at the dentist. I will next return to the dentist and hygienist in six months. I was welcomed back to work and told that I look rested and as if I had a tan.

Tuesday 22nd November 2016

Dear Yvonne,
This morning I went to work and had supervision with manager. My partner is still on annual leave from work and today I had the first phone conversation with her since returning from Barbados. This was the first evening, since Sunday that I was able to devote some quality time with my beloved son James.

Wednesday 23rd November 2016

Dear Yvonne,
Today I did a nine to five shift at work. We had our team meeting this afternoon. This evening my son and I attended the LGBT+ Conservatives Christmas drinks at the Punch Tavern in Fleet Street, near St Paul's Cathedral.

Thursday 24th November 2016

Dear Yvonne,
Today I arrived at work for 14:30hrs. While I was at work, my son communicated to me that he was going to be spending this evening at the home of a Rudolf Steiner school friend. I arrived home at approximately 23:30hrs and my son came home at around 00:15hrs.

Friday 25th November 2016

Dear Yvonne,
Today is my day off. I spent most of it resting in bed and communicating with my son and partner. This morning my son had a two hour driving lesson.

Saturday 26th November 2016

Dear Yvonne,
At noon today I attended a Lambeth wide Black Wellbeing Partnership mental health steering committee, community member interview at the Black Cultural Archives in Windrush Square; after I sent in a video application for the position.

Sunday 27th November 2016

Dear Yvonne,
This morning I started work at 07:00. After work I met with my dear old friend Birgit Rapp. I also received an email today to say that the interview which I did yesterday was successful and the first

meeting which I will attend is at 18:00hrs on Tuesday 13th December 2016.

Monday 28th November 2016

Dear Yvonne,
Today was another work day and I spent some time in the IWM - Imperial War Museum.

Tuesday 29th November 2016

Dear Yvonne,
Today we had a power cut at work. This caused our gas supply to fail and resulted in staff and clients spending time standing outside of the building until the boiler room was checked.

Wednesday 30th November 2016

Dear Yvonne,
Today I am very disappointed because on my arrival home from work this evening, in preparation to attending the Vauxhall Conservatives drinks and the 50:50 Parliament's launch of the 'Ask Her to Stand' campaign. I received a letter confirming that I was not successful with my 28th October 2016 Cambridge Conservative PAB - Parliamentary Assessment Board test. So, as it stands, at the moment I cannot stand for my Conservative Party to be a Parliamentary Candidate. I'm going to bed!

Thursday 1st December 2016

Dear Yvonne,
Today there was a small fire started in the kitchen at work. The building had to be evacuated and the fire brigade was called.

Friday 2nd December 2016

Dear Yvonne,
Today I arrived at work for 07:00hrs. It was a non-stop type of working day, as usual. It makes the day go faster. When I got home this evening, joy of all joys, my son had already made a start on his domestic chores. After settling in, I removed my items from several of my chest of drawers so that I son could place his belongings in it. Then I supported my son to use the washing machine to wash his clothes.

Saturday 3rd December 2016

Dear Yvonne,
Today is my day off. I spent the morning in bed. I spent most of the time creating a keynote powerpoint slide presentation for my forthcoming Slough Baylis Court Girls School Tuesday 14th December 2016 Stonewall School Role Model talk. This afternoon I spent shopping and in the evening I did my washing.

Sunday 4th December 2016

Dear Yvonne,
Today was a work day. This morning I attended a
Quaker Meeting for Worship at my local Brixton
and Streatham Friends Meeting House.

Monday 5th December 2016

Dear Yvonne,
This morning, I had a lie-in and then went for a flat
white coffee at my local Ritzy Bar, before going to
work. I spent time speaking with my partner and
this evening, my beloved son James told me that
he had enjoyed his driving lesson.

Tuesday 6th December 2016

Dear Yvonne,
Today before work, I went to my local Ritzy Bar for
a flat white coffee.

Wednesday 7th December 2016

Dear Yvonne,
Today before work, I stopped off at my GP to
renew my 'Stella' anti-psychotic mental health
prescription. I also secured my online doctors ID
details and will register when I find some time.
Once I arrived at work, I was in time for my
supervision with Sydney, my Lead Manager. She
keeps me on point.

Thursday 8th December 2016

Dear Yvonne,
Today at work, my son's social worker rang me. I was just in the midst of a starting a meeting with a psychiatrist and one of my clients; so I wasn't able to speak long. I said that I would return the call but forgot. This evening on my way home from work, I stopped off at my local Sainsbury's.

Friday 9th December 2016

Dear Yvonne,
Today was my day off. I was shattered and spent most of it sleeping on and off in bed. Every now and again, I could hear my son laughing about something that he was viewing on line and he would come to share the joke with me. My son has now learnt how to independently use the oven and today shared some chicken nuggets with he had baked. My partner said that she was proud of him. My son's social worker rang me today and has arranged a 'Review' for my son for 10am this Monday at International House with my son. Today I received my Lambeth Black Wellbeing Partnership Steering Committee minutes and agenda for the forthcoming meeting this Tuesday evening.

Saturday 10th December 2016

Dear Yvonne,
Today is my day off. I spent most of the morning sleeping. Then I went for a flat white coffee in the Ritzy Bar. I then went food shopping at M&S. On

my return home I cleaned the kitchen and the bathroom and washed some clothes in the washing machine. I then registered my ID for my doctors, downloaded the app onto my phone and made an online appointment for a Health Review with my GP for 10am on Tuesday morning.

Sunday 11th December 2016

Dear Yvonne,
Today I was back at work for 7am, after a sleepless night. For some reason, I just could hardly sleep. On my return home I have taken a bath and I am going straight to bed.

Monday 12th December 2016

Dear Yvonne,
At 10am this morning before work, my son and I attended a social service review with the social worker and the IRO Independent Reviewing Officer at International House. I was there for over two hours. The next review will be Friday 5th May 2016.

Tuesday 13th December 2016

Dear Yvonne,
Today is my annual leave day. This morning, I collected my anti-psychotic medication from the local pharmacy. Then I went to my GP - General Practitioner at Brixton Water Lane Surgery and had my annual medical checkup. I am now

weighing nearly sixteen stones. 100kg and my blood pressure was slightly high. I followed my GP appointment by going to Dulwich Hospital to get my blood taken. Next I stopped off at Camberwell Magistrates Court in Camberwell Green. This is because I am in the process of applying to become a magistrate and Camberwell is my local court. I will start attending the court next week Monday morning at 9am to 1pm in Court one and two in the public gallery. This evening, I attended the Lambeth BWP - Black Wellbeing Partnership Steering Committee, which was Chaired by Cllr Jacqui Dyer as a Community Member for the first time. It was held at High Trees in Tulse Hill.

Wednesday 14th December 2016

Dear Yvonne,
Today I did a Stonewall Role Model LGBT presentation at the all girls Baylis Court School in Slough for year seven. Approximately two hundred and fifty girls attended my talk and keynote powerpoint presentation. The girls appeared engaged and asked lots of questions and I think that the event went well.

Thursday 15th December 2016

Dear Yvonne,
Today I was on a Client Specialism Day at work. This means that I get to spend additional time with my clients and on my admin. After I finished work, I received a message from my beloved son requesting a fish and chips supper. Today my domestic bliss with my partner developed a little

rockiness for a few hours. However we resolved it and was lovey-dovey before bedtime.

Friday 16th December 2016

Dear Yvonne,
This morning, before doing an extra shift for this week at work, I went to Camberwell Green Magistrates Court and sat in the public gallery of Court Two and Court One. I heard several cases.

Saturday 17th December 2016

Dear Yvonne,
Today was my day off. I spent the morning sleeping. I received a few Xmas cards in the post today. I also went to the Ritzy Bar and sat sipping a flat white coffee and communicating with my partner. I followed this with some shopping in M&S and then I went to a travel agents in Victoria to speculate on a possible holiday in September 2017. This evening I spent in my son's company.

Sunday 18th December 2016

Dear Yvonne,
Today I was on Welcoming Duties at my local Quaker Meeting for Worship. After the end of the meeting, I briefly stopped off at the Ritzy Bar. I have been trying to drink at least eight glasses of water each day. On average I manage seven to eight glasses a day over the period of a week. Today when I got to work, I decided that I would bring my new years resolution forward and start

riding my Brompton bicycle to and from work from tomorrow. I have also started a new blog http://www.heathenmassive.blogspot.com where I publicly record my progress.

Monday 19th December 2016

Dear Yvonne,
Today I psyched myself up and prepared my bike then walked to the Ritzy Bar with my bike and sipped a flat white coffee then cycled from The Ritzy Bar in Brixton to Pret in Waterloo Road. It took about me about forty-five minutes. I got to work without a struggle and then in the evening I cycled from my workplace to Brixton Police Station. That was a little quicker.

Tuesday 20th December 2016

Dear Yvonne,
This morning I received a non urgent letter from my GP Surgery. They want me to make an appointment to see them regarding the results from my latest blood test.

Wednesday 21st December 2016

Dear Yvonne,
Today I am starting to feel a bit of a struggle with the cycling routine. My cycling time has been improving. Today It was my work Christmas dinner. This took place in Camberwell. I left my bike at work, attended the dinner; collected it and then cycled homeward.

Thursday 22nd December 2016

Dear Yvonne,
This morning I attended a BWP-Black Wellbeing
Partnership meeting at Health-Watch's offices at
We Are 336 Brixton Road and then cycled to work.

Friday 23rd December 2016

Dear Yvonne,
Today was my final cycling day for this week. I am
shattered after a day of visiting the public gallery
of court two, of the London Inner City Crown Court
in Elephant and Castle with one of my clients.

Saturday 24th December 2016

Dear Yvonne,
Today is the first of my forthcoming three days off.
This is also the first time in eleven years that I will
have spent it with my beloved son James. I am
overcome with joy!!

Sunday 25th December 2016

Dear Yvonne,
I stayed awake until about 06:30hrs today talking
to my son about his Christmas present and
communicating with my partner and Birgit. I was
slightly late for my Quaker meeting today; but was
glad to have been present. I walked there and
back. I spent most of the day listening to music
and trying to sort out my bedroom, while my son
slept.

Monday 26th December 2016

Dear Yvonne,
Today is my annual leave day off. I went to have a flat white coffee in my favorite watering hole. My body feels recovered from the cycling which I did prior to Christmas. I spent some time with my beloved son and completed some life admin.

Tuesday 27th December 2016

Dear Yvonne,
Today I was back at work. I cycled and my time was fifteen minutes shorter than when I first began my commuter cycling. I didn't feel tired.

Wednesday 28th December 2016

Dear Yvonne.
Today I again cycled to and from work. I didn't feel too tired but it was cold and my fingertips were frozen by the time I arrived home. I took a lovely hot candlelit bubble bath and went to straight to bed.

Thursday 29th December 2016

Dear Yvonne,
Today is my day off and I spent most of the morning asleep in bed. I then went to the Ritzy Bar and sat sipping a flat white coffee. This afternoon and evening I spent some quality time with my beloved son James and also communicated with my partner; while completing some life admin.

Friday 30th December 2016

Dear Yvonne,
This morning my son did the grocery shopping
and spent within budget. Today is my day off. I
spent my day relaxing and communicating with my
son and partner.

Saturday 31st December 2016

Dear Yvonne,
Today was a work day. I cycled to and from work.
I am still posting to my blog. Today signals the
start of six consecutive work days.

Sunday 1st January 2017

Dear Yvonne,
Today I was at work for a 7am start. I continued
my resolution and cycled to and from work.

Monday 2nd January 2017

Dear Yvonne,
Today was a bank holiday and I was working a
shift with my manager. Today my son cooked
some turkey mince and pasta and saved some for
me to eat, for when I came home from work this
evening.

Tuesday 3rd January 2017

Dear Yvonne,
Today my son cooked scrambled eggs for himself.
In addition, my line manager came back to work
from her leave and has given up smoking
cigarettes. She has made an agreement with me
to stop smoking, if I cycle. It was an extra busy
and stressful shift. Today was the first time which I
cycled from my home to work for a shift and then
cycled home after a shift from my work. I was
shattered by the time I arrived home and took a
hot candlelit bubble bath and then went to bed.

Wednesday 4th January 2017

Dear Yvonne,
Today on the way to work, my Brompton bicycle
chain came off and started to slip when I placed it
on. I handed my bike in to Brixton Cycles and took
the bus to work. I had supervision at work today
and after handover and a team meeting, I took a
bus to Brixton Cycles and collected my bicycle. It
cost me thirty pounds to have a new chain and
sprockets fitted. I cycled home and spent the
evening playing computer games with my son and
communicating with my partner.

Thursday 5th January 2017

Dear Yvonne,
Today I cycled from my home to work for my shift
and home again at the end of it. I felt quite tired
today. I spent some time communicating with my
son and partner and I was glad to soak in a lovely

hot candlelit bubble bath and doing some life admin and going to bed.

Friday 6th January 2017

Dear Yvonne,
Today is my day off. This morning I attended a Lambeth BWP, International Amnesty design Meeting, held by Champion Agency at the Piano Club, at 9, Brighton Terrace, in Brixton. This afternoon, I went for a falafel meal in Camberwell with Birgit, my best female friend. Her treat!!

Saturday 7th January 2017

Dear Yvonne,
This morning I struggled to get out of my bed to be cycle and get to work for a 07:00hr start. I managed to cycle to work in just under thirty-three minutes and I arrived home again in just under thirty-two minutes. My beloved son James was cooking again this evening. He seems to be turning into a little Gordon Ramsey!

Sunday 8th January 2017

Dear Yvonne,
This morning before work, I was on Welcoming duties at my local Brixton and Streatham Quaker Friends Meeting House. It was here were I first heard that Quaker member Helen Fensterheim, had died this past Thursday 5th January 2017. Although Helen lived in my Brixton, Coldharbour Ward, she had usually voted for the Green Party

had also proposed my nomination so that I could stand for Councillor for my Conservative Party.

Monday 9th January 2017

Dear Yvonne,
Today I was again at work. I cycled from my workplace to my home this evening in thirty minutes and thirteen seconds!

Tuesday 10th January 2017

Dear Yvonne,
Today is my annual leave from work. I spent this morning communicating with my partner and then watching preceding in Court one and two of Camberwell Green Magistrates Court. I witnessed criminal damage, minor assault and motor cases. This afternoon, my beloved son James enjoyed another driving lesson. This evening I am to attend a Lambeth Black Wellbeing Partnership Steering Committee meeting at High Trees in Tulse Hill.

Wednesday 11th January 2017

Dear Yvonne,
Today was my second annual leave day off from work. I spent some time this afternoon, being debriefed about my prior attendance on Friday 28th October 2016 PAB - Parliamentary Assessment Board; at my main Conservative party headquarters. I am so deeply disappointed that I did not pass. I have so much work to day and so many people that need what I have to offer. This afternoon, I contacted CWO -

Conservative Women's Organisation and my local DWNCA - Dulwich and West Norwood Conservative Association to start the process to trying to stand for my local Coldharbour Ward, in Lambeth's Brixton / Loughborough Junction as a Councillor at the forthcoming 2018 local election.

Thursday 12th January 2017

Dear Yvonne,
Today was another work day. I cycled to work and seem to be creating a real rhythm but this evening after work, I cycled for one kilometre and then walked the rest because it was dark, cold, wet and windy in addition to being slippery due to sleet. So instead of taking approximately thirty minutes; it took me just over an hour to get home from work.

Friday 13th January 2017

Dear Yvonne,
Today is my day off. I felt a bit stiff but I still managed to attend my Lodge Adelaide Litten No.23 Women Freemasonry practice and had a great time.

Saturday 14th January 2017

Dear Yvonne,
Today is also my day off. I spent all day at home and most of the day in bed. My beloved son and I chatted to each other, ate slept and relaxed. We also spent time communicating with my partner.

Sunday 15th January 2017

Dear Yvonne,
This morning I cycled in the rain to work and arrived approximately two minutes before I was due to start for 07:00hrs. I had a very busy day at work, as usual and I cycled home in the rain. I was slower than usual so I then walked to and from M&S in Brixton, where I purchased a few perishables for me and my beloved son James. I am now going to have a lovely long soak in a hot candlelit bubble bath and then I'll relax and read a book.

Monday 16th January 2017

Dear Yvonne,
Today I was extraordinarily busy at work. The shift went by so fast and I didn't even stop to have a break; because we were one worker short.

Tuesday 17th January 2017

Dear Yvonne,
Today at work, we had a full complement of staff and we were worked off our feet. I did manage to get a thirty minute break and spent some time talking to Birgit, my best female friend on the phone.

Wednesday 18th January 2017

Dear Yvonne,
This morning I was so tired that I cycled to work, five minutes slower than usual. In addition I

missed my fortnightly supervision because my manager was very busy writing her quarterly reports. We spent a long time in meetings today and I left work late. It was almost 20:30 when I left the hostel.

Thursday 19th January 2017

Dear Yvonne,
This morning I arrived to work at approximately 08:30hrs. On the commute in I found myself in the company of many other cyclists; all riding faster than me!

Friday 20th January 2017

Dear Yvonne,
Today is my day off. I spent the morning resting in bed. This afternoon I got on with some domestic chores. This evening I attended a Freemason's event with my Lodge.

Saturday 21st January 2017

Dear Yvonne,
Today is my day off. I spent all day at home with my beloved son James.

Sunday 22nd January 2017

Dear Yvonne,
This morning, I was woke up too late to go to my local Brixton and Streatham Quaker meeting for worship. I cycled to work this afternoon. It was a bit cold and icy.

Monday 23rd January 2017

Dear Yvonne,
Today I worked a late shift. I left my beloved son James at home and cycled to work. I was an extra busy shift because we were one worker down.

Tuesday 24th January 2017

Dear Yvonne,
This morning before work, I attended a meeting on behalf of the BWP to assess the progress made with the logo. I was heartily enthusiastic about one of the selections.

Wednesday 25th January 2017

Dear Yvonne,
Today it was so cold during my cycle to work that my finger tips hurt. I did manage to cycle to and from work and made sure that I had a lovely hot candlelit bubble bath on my return home.

Thursday 26th January 2017

Dear Yvonne
Today it was zero degrees, but I still cycled to and from work. My finger tips were blue!! Today my son's social worker rang me and told me that he thought my son is avoiding him. My son's social worker has made an appointment to come to my abode tomorrow at 16.00 to visit my son in addition to paying his week's subsistence money. I told the social worker that it is my day off tomorrow and I have an appointment with my GP at 16.40hrs. I addition I am taking James to sign up at the local gym at Brixton Recreation Centre and booking an appointment for him with the hygienist. This evening my son told me that he will be having a driving lesson at the time that his social worker wants to visit. This evening I did not attend my DWNCA Executive Council meeting.

Friday 27th January 2017

Dear Yvonne,
Today is my day off. I spent it paying bills, enrolling my son onto a gym subscription, food shopping, booking CWO-Conservative Women's Organisation courses and workshops, booking extra driving lessons for my son, confirming my booking at a Brompton maintenance course, booking a hygienist appointment for my son at our local dentist, confirming a booking at the Karibu Centre for next month's Coldharbour and Herne Hill Wards AGM. I also found time to have a flat white coffee and a muffin at my favourite watering

hole i.e. The Ritzy Bar.; Get home in time to meet with my son's social worker, while my son was on a driving lesson and then visited my GP and found out that I have a cholesterol level of 6.4. I then found time to get on a bus to Clapham to order and collect a Burger fries and milkshake for my son from GBK Gourmet Burger Kitchen and go for my LGBT+ Conservative friend's birthday drinks in Camden.

Saturday 28th January 2017

Dear Yvonne,
Today is my day off. This morning, my beloved son James independently did the weekly food shopping at our local Sainsbury's. I spent the day at CCHQ-Conservative Central Headquarters, in Westminster on a course organised by CWO-Conservative Women's Organisation. I learnt loads.

Sunday 29th January 2017

Dear Yvonne,
Today I took one day of annual leave. My beloved son James independently did some food shopping at M&S in Brixton and started a spring clean on his living area in our abode. I attended a one day Brompton Maintenance course in Bermondsey at the offices of Cycle Training UK. I got covered in grease and learnt loads.

Tuesday 14th February 2017

Dear Yvonne,
Today is Valentines Day and I have spoken with
my darling Julian, who is in Jamaica. I am thinking
about our recent holiday together in Barbados. I
have left my beloved son James in bed and made
my way to my favourite watering hole 'The Ritzy
Bar' in my local Brixton Coldharbour Ward. I am
sipping on a flat white coffee, while reading my
email. Today I received a response from my
signed petition wanting President Trump here in
the United Kingdom. In addition I received a
response from Helen Hayes MP, my Dulwich &
West Norwood Member of Parliament, to confirm
her support for LGBT - Lesbian, Gay, Bisexual &
Transgender issues. This evening I will be
attending a meeting as a Black Lesbian
Community Member of the Lambeth BWP - Black
Wellbeing Partnership Steering Committee; which
will take place at the Black Cultural Archives. The
Lambeth BWP Steering Committee is chaired by
Councillor Jacqui Dyer MBE and has been formed
for the mental health and wellbeing of African, and
African Caribbean who work, rest and play in the
borough of Lambeth. I am enjoying my day of
annual leave and having thoughts of trying to
publish this memoir via Chipmunkapublishing. I
have declared my intentions to stand for
Councillor in Brixton Coldharbour Ward, my local
neighbourhood and also have a AGM - Annual
General Meeting to attend for Dulwich & West
Norwood Coldharbour and Herne Hill Ward
Branch, on the 21st of February 2017. It was

conveyed to me that I was missed at this month's Executive Council meeting of the DWNCA - Dulwich & West Norwood Conservative Association; However I have now submitted my Council Forms. How wonderful it is to be in the middle of this February LGBT History Month 2017.

Wednesday 15th February 2017

Dear Yvonne,
Today I had supervision with Sydney, my Waterloo Project, Thames Reach manager. I mentioned that when I was assaulted earlier this week in the hostel and reported it to the police; and they had informed me that if it happens again, he will be arrested. I had experienced a lack of trust in that client. I thanked Sydney for her risk assessment and explained that I have been feeling under the weather, hence distancing myself. I discussed the fact that I have spoken to Primrose , my GP+ worker and have made an appointment for next Friday with her to visit the Effra Mosaic Club House for lunch. My manager then asked me to take take the next few days off work and return on Monday. I took the bus home and stopped off in my local neighbourhood Bar for a flat white coffee; where I used my Apple laptop to create a keynote presentation for my Stonewall school role position.

Lightning Source UK Ltd.
Milton Keynes UK
UKOW05f1410070617
302877UK00001B/22/P